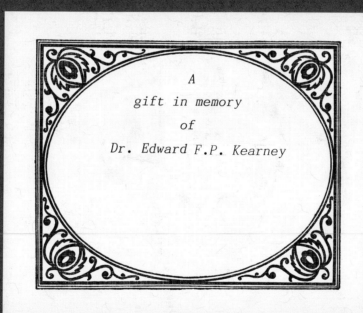

The Shadow War

By the Editors of Time-Life Books

Alexandria, Virginia

TIME
LIFE ®

Time-Life Books is a division of
Time Life Inc., a wholly owned subsidiary of

The Time Inc. Book Company
Time-Life Books

Managing Editor: Thomas H. Flaherty
Director of Editorial Resources:
Elise D. Ritter-Clough
Director of Photography and Research:
John Conrad Weiser
Editorial Board: Dale M. Brown, Roberta Conlan,
Laura Foreman, Lee Hassig, Jim Hicks, Blaine
Marshall, Rita Thievon Mullin, Henry Woodhead

PUBLISHER: Joseph J. Ward

Associate Publisher: Ann Mirabito
Editorial Director: Russell B. Adams, Jr.
Marketing Director: Anne C. Everhart
Director of Design: Louis Klein
Production Manager: Prudence G. Harris
Supervisor of Quality Control: James King

Editorial Operations
Production: Celia Beattie
Library: Louise D. Forstall
Computer Composition: Deborah G. Tait
(Manager), Monika D. Thayer,
Janet Barnes Syring, Lillian Daniels

The Third Reich

SERIES EDITOR: Henry Woodhead
Series Administrators: Jane Edwin,
Philip Brandt George (acting)
Editorial Staff for *The Shadow War:*
Senior Art Director: Raymond Ripper
Picture Editor: Jane Coughran
Text Editor: John Newton
Writer: Stephanie A. Lewis
Associate Editors/Research: Oobie Gleysteen,
Karen Monks
Assistant Editor/Research: Maggie Debelius
Assistant Art Director: Lorraine D. Rivard
Copy Coordinator: Anne Farr
Picture Coordinator: Jennifer Iker
Editorial Assistants: Jayne A. L. Dover,
Alan Schager

Special Contributors: Ronald H. Bailey,
John Clausen, Lydia Preston Hicks, Peter Pocock,
Brian C. Pohanka, Curtis W. Prendergast, David
S. Thomson (text); Martha Lee Beckington,
Barbara Fleming, Marilyn Murphy Terrell
(research); Roy Nanovic (index)

Correspondents: Elisabeth Kraemer-Singh
(Bonn), Christine Hinze (London), Christina
Lieberman (New York), Maria Vincenza Aloisi
(Paris), Ann Natanson (Rome). Valuable
assistance was also provided by: Mehmet Ali
Kislali (Ankara), Pavle Svabic (Belgrade), Angie
Lemmer (Bonn), Maria Estenssoro (Buenos
Aires), Nihal Tamraz (Cairo), Judy Aspinall
(London), Trini Bandrés, Michael Gore (Madrid),
Sasha Isachenko (Moscow), Wibo Vandelinde,
Rene Dessing (Netherlands), Elizabeth Brown
(New York), John Maier (Rio de Janeiro), Ann
Wise (Rome), Traudl Lessing (Vienna).

Other Publications:

TIME-LIFE LIBRARY OF CURIOUS AND UNUSUAL FACTS
AMERICAN COUNTRY
VOYAGE THROUGH THE UNIVERSE
THE TIME-LIFE GARDENER'S GUIDE
MYSTERIES OF THE UNKNOWN
TIME FRAME
FIX IT YOURSELF
FITNESS, HEALTH & NUTRITION
SUCCESSFUL PARENTING
HEALTHY HOME COOKING
UNDERSTANDING COMPUTERS
LIBRARY OF NATIONS
THE ENCHANTED WORLD
THE KODAK LIBRARY OF CREATIVE PHOTOGRAPHY
GREAT MEALS IN MINUTES
THE CIVIL WAR
PLANET EARTH
COLLECTOR'S LIBRARY OF THE CIVIL WAR
THE EPIC OF FLIGHT
THE GOOD COOK
WORLD WAR II
HOME REPAIR AND IMPROVEMENT
THE OLD WEST

For information on and a full description of any
of the Time-Life Books series listed above, please
call 1-800-621-7026 or write:
Reader Information
Time-Life Customer Service
P.O. Box C-32068
Richmond, Virginia 23261-2068

The Cover: Wearing an Italian lieutenant's hat with
his own navy overcoat, Admiral Wilhelm Canaris
presents an enigmatic facade to the world. As director of the Abwehr, the espionage branch of the
German military, he skirted hurdles thrown up by
rival spy chieftains and transformed a minor agency into the Third Reich's premier source of foreign
intelligence.

This volume is one of a series that chronicles
the rise and eventual fall of Nazi Germany. Other
books in the series include:
The SS
Fists of Steel
Storming to Power
The New Order
The Reach for Empire
Lightning War
Wolf Packs
Conquest of the Balkans
Afrikakorps
The Center of the Web
Barbarossa
War on the High Seas
The Twisted Dream
The Road to Stalingrad

First printing. Printed in U.S.A.

Published simultaneously in Canada.
School and library distribution by Silver Burdett
Company, Morristown, New Jersey 07960.

TIME-LIFE is a trademark of Time Warner Inc.
U.S.A.

**Library of Congress Cataloging in
Publication Data**
The Shadow war / by the editors of
Time-Life Books.
    p.   cm. — (The Third Reich)
Includes bibliographical references and index.
ISBN 0-8094-7008-X (trade)
ISBN 0-8094-7009-8 (lib. bdg.)
    1. World War, 1939-1945—Secret service.
2. World War, 1939-1945—Diplomatic history.
I. Time-Life Books. II. Series.
D810.S7S43 1991   940.54'85—dc20   90-48517

General Consultants

Col. John R. Elting, USA (Ret.), former associate professor at West Point, has written
or edited some twenty books, including
*Swords around a Throne, The Superstrate-
gists,* and *American Army Life,* as well as
Battles for Scandinavia in the Time-Life
Books World War II series. He was chief con-
sultant to the Time-Life series The Civil War.

Charles V. P. von Luttichau is an associate
at the U.S. Army Center of Military History in
Washington, D.C., and coauthor of *Com-
mand Decision* and *Great Battles.* From 1937
to 1945, he served in the German air force
and taught at the air force academy in Berlin.
After the war, he emigrated to the United
States and was a historian in the Office of the
Chief of Military History, Department of the
Army, from 1951 to 1986, when he retired.

Contents

Shadow Legions

Hitler's Reich spawned a welter of organizations that conducted espionage and counterespionage. As was often the case in the Nazi bureaucracy, these secret services rarely cooperated with one another and frequently worked at cross-purposes. The leaders of these clandestine organizations were complex, ambitious men who vied for power, scarcely hesitating to discredit a rival in the Machiavellian struggle for supremacy in the German shadow world.

One of the spymasters, Admiral Wilhelm Canaris, with his rumpled uniform, eccentric mannerisms, and lisping voice, seemed an unlikely chief of the Abwehr, the military intelligence section of the Wehrmacht. A pill-popping hypochondriac who wore heavy winter clothing year round, Canaris harbored an irrational dislike of tall people and those with small ears. Virtually estranged from his wife and children and brusque with

subordinates, Canaris nonetheless fretted obsessively over the health of his pets. "My dachshund is discreet and will never betray me," he once told a fellow officer. "I cannot say that of any human being."

Despite his personal oddities, the intellectually gifted Canaris proved to be a more-than-capable director of the Abwehr. Under his leadership, the intelligence network's staff increased tenfold. Canaris attained sweeping powers as well as autonomy from competing organizations such as Reinhard Heydrich's Sicherheitsdienst (SD), the secret service of the SS. Fond of traveling in mufti to interact personally with agents in the field, Canaris gained the invaluable respect of the powerful SS chief, Heinrich Himmler, who regarded him as a "born spy."

As the war progressed, however, Canaris became increasingly disillusioned with the Nazi hierarchy and eventually found his position intolerable. His former protégé Heydrich proved a duplicitous and dangerous adversary who relentlessly sought to undermine the admiral's authority and absorb the Abwehr into the sinister empire of the SS.

Dressed in his naval frock coat, Admiral Canaris, who disliked wearing his medals, poses for a formal portrait (right).

In 1936 Canaris (right) meets with Heinrich Himmler (front) and Propaganda Minister Joseph Goebbels (center) in Berlin.

Canaris, who preferred civilian clothes to his naval uniform, walks Motte, his favorite Arabian

A Cold and Calculating Spymaster

As head of intelligence and security for the SS, Reinhard Heydrich was so ruthless that his own subordinates dubbed him the Blond Beast. Admiral Canaris considered Heydrich a "brutal fanatic," while his close associate Walter Schellenberg likened him to a "predatory animal," who "could carry injustice to the point of extreme cruelty."

Heydrich, however, was a man of contradictions. He loved music and played the violin skillfully. Introverted and socially awkward, with a gangly figure and a high-pitched voice, he nonetheless became a skilled fencer, a crack shot, and a cross-country runner.

A notorious philanderer, an inveterate pub-crawler, and the founder of Salon Kitty, the official SD brothel, Heydrich fostered the image of a loving husband and father. And despite the rumor that he had Jewish ancestry, he was exalted by Himmler as the very model of Aryan superiority.

Although he cut an elegant figure in his SS uniform *(right)*, Walter Schellenberg shared Canaris's penchant for traveling incognito. Schellenberg *(left, in black hat)* was secretly photographed as he stepped from a commercial airliner at Lisbon. In 1939, the ambitious officer divorced his first wife, a seamstress, to marry a woman who was more prominent socially *(below)*.

The Man with an Ear at Every Wall

At age thirty-one, SS Major Walter Schellenberg took over the foreign intelligence wing of Heydrich's burgeoning espionage and security empire. The hardworking officer possessed boyish good looks and a quiet, unassuming manner; a contemporary found him a "man of clever and winning ways."

But Schellenberg's amiable exterior masked a ruthless ambition. Suspicious and cunning, he habitually spied on his own agents, one of whom observed, "He had an ear at every wall." It was Schellenberg who presented Himmler, the head of the SS, with evidence that Admiral Canaris had been disloyal to the Reich in 1943. Schellenberg later arrested Canaris for his involvement in the plot to assassinate Hitler and assumed control of the admiral's former domain.

Reinhard Gehlen, the brilliant intelligence chief of Foreign Armies East, poses with a group of fellow officers *(right)*, and at his desk at FHO headquarters in Zossen. In 1944, he visited the training camp of the pro-German Russian Army of Liberation *(below)*. Dour and secretive, Gehlen craved anonymity and was rarely photographed.

The Army's Faceless Spy Chief

Though widely regarded as the most efficient of all German military intelligence operatives, Lieut. Colonel Reinhard Gehlen was a shadowy figure whom a journalist once called a "faceless man." Born to a middle-class Prussian family, he commanded a battery of artillery in the prewar Reichswehr before becoming senior aide to General Franz Halder, chief of the High Command of the Army.

In April 1942, Gehlen was placed in charge of Foreign Armies East, or FHO, the section of the high command that collected military intelligence in eastern Europe. A demanding taskmaster, he assembled an intelligence team of energetic young officers who, by carefully sifting all available data, compiled a remarkably accurate picture of Soviet forces that evaluated enemy strength and combat effectiveness in minute detail.

In the Service of Secrecy

Precisely at 8:00 a.m. on January 2, 1935, a slight, gnomelike figure, wearing the uniform of a navy captain, passed through the entrance of no. 72-76 Tirpitz-Ufer, an imposing sandstone building in Berlin's central Tiergarten district. Since the days of Emperor William II, the structure had been part of a vast complex of War Ministry offices. Down the street, it connected internally with a row of formerly elegant town houses acquired by the government, and it was linked, by rear corridors and courtyards, to the sprawling armed forces headquarters around the corner on Bendlerstrasse.

No more than five feet four inches tall, the man had silver hair, bushy eyebrows, and a slow walk that made him appear older than his forty-eight years; his heavy nose and drooping jowls gave him the sad-faced mien of a bloodhound. Once inside, he made his way through a maze of staircases and dim hallways to the Fuchsbau, or Fox Den, a warren of former bedrooms, dining rooms, living rooms, and kitchens that now served as headquarters for the Abwehr, the War Ministry's intelligence and counterintelligence service. The legendary Wilhelm Franz Canaris was about to begin his first day as Adolf Hitler's chief spymaster.

Although the history of German military spying extends back before the time of Frederick the Great in the eighteenth century, the agency Canaris was taking over was only fifteen years old. Its roots lay in the turbulent autumn days of 1918 when the provisional Reichswehr, the Weimar's defense force, and the Freikorps, volunteer paramilitary units that sprang up following Germany's defeat in World War I, responded to the disorder by purging their ranks of Communist spies and left-wing revolutionaries. The first director, Major Friedrich Gempp of the army, moved the fledgling spy agency, named Amt Ausland/Abwehr, or Foreign Office/Defense, into the Tirpitz-Ufer headquarters in 1920. Soon, it united with the Heeresstatistische Abteilung, or Army Statistical Section, which served the Truppenamt, or Troop Department, the organization that had replaced Germany's outlawed General Staff.

As the Communist threat receded and the Weimar Republic stabilized,

Erich Glaser, a former United States Army Air Corps private *(left)*, and Otto Voss, an aircraft factory worker, both German-born Americans and Abwehr spies, leave federal court in New York City on October 18, 1938, the fourth day of their trial for conspiring to steal United States military secrets. Glaser received two years in prison; Voss, six.

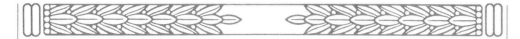

the Abwehr focused on Germany's foreign rivals. Gempp set up outstations on the eastern frontier, where the large Polish army posed a threat to national security. In 1928, the agency's authority increased dramatically. Kurt von Schleicher, chief of the armed forces division in the Reichswehr, placed the naval intelligence service under its aegis and made it a separate bureau responsible to him. Four years later, despite grumblings from army officers, who considered military intelligence their exclusive preserve, Schleicher put a navy man, Captain Konrad Patzig, in charge.

The appointment proved a stroke of brilliance. An excellent organizer, Patzig expanded the Abwehr's network of agents abroad and mounted an aggressive counterespionage campaign at home aimed at concealing Germany's secret rearmament schemes. But his agents were frustrated by their lack of authority to make actual arrests. When Adolf Hitler came to power in 1933, Patzig and his spy hunters welcomed the rise of Hermann Göring's Geheime Staatspolizei (Secret State Police Department), or Gestapo. The Nazi organization seemed to fit the bill as the powerful enforcement partner the Abwehr needed to complement its investigations.

The two agencies began collaborating and soon achieved a major triumph. In February of 1934, they smashed a Polish spy ring headed by a former cavalry officer named Juri von Sosnowski. Well-financed and apparently irresistible to women, Sosnowski charmed his way into Berlin society circles. Over the course of several years, he gained access to some of the nation's best-kept military secrets by seducing the private secretaries of War Ministry officials, then coercing them into becoming his accomplices. A jealous countess finally tipped off the Abwehr, which infiltrated Sosnowski's network and brought in the Gestapo to make the arrests.

A few months later, however, Hitler forced Göring to cede his police fiefdom to Heinrich Himmler's elite Schutzstaffel (Protection Squad), or SS, the Nazi party's black-uniformed political watchdogs, and the warm relations between the two agencies ended. The Gestapo was now an arm of the SS's own intelligence apparatus, the new Sicherheitsdienst (Security Service), or SD, headed by the feared and ruthless Reinhard Heydrich, who had created the organization according to the Himmler dictum: "The SD unmasks the adversaries of National Socialist ideas." As part of his master plan to create an all-encompassing, national surveillance system, Heydrich set his sights on the Abwehr.

Patzig refused to allow the War Ministry's small, highly professional bureau to be gobbled up by the Nazis. He repeatedly rebuffed Heydrich's badgerings for classified information, including a list of Germany's secret munitions factories, and waited for an opportunity to counterattack.

It came with the Blood Purge of June 30, 1934, the cynical assassinations

The Polish intelligence agent Juri von Sosnowski *(far right)* dines at a fashionable Berlin restaurant with Benita von Falkenhayn, a German divorcée who was one of his many mistresses and a member of his spy ring. Caught by the Abwehr, Sosnowski was exchanged for four German agents arrested in Poland; Falkenhayn was condemned to death.

planned by Hitler to curtail the growing power of his own brown-shirted Sturmabteilung (Storm Detachment), or SA, led by Ernst Röhm. Zealous SS execution squads deliberately overstepped orders and murdered several army officers, including Kurt von Schleicher. Patzig pinned the excesses on Heydrich and lobbied with Minister of War General Werner von Blomberg to press Himmler for Heydrich's dismissal. Instead, the pro-Nazi Blomberg turned against Patzig and forced him to resign. Asked by the commander in chief of the navy, Admiral Erich Raeder, to recommend a successor, Patzig suggested Canaris.

At the time, Canaris's career was in total eclipse. Raeder did not trust him. He considered Canaris too mysterious and political, sharing the view of Karl Dönitz, the future leader of Hitler's U-boat force, who scornfully referred to his former commanding officer as "the man with many souls in his breast." Just three months earlier, in September 1934, Raeder had exiled Canaris to a dead-end, land-based command on the Baltic, expecting the middle-aged officer to go quietly into retirement. But because of the interservice rivalry, Raeder backed Patzig's choice. The alternative was to hand the Abwehr directorship over to an army man at a critical moment in history—just as the Führer was about to begin testing the resolve of World War I's victorious Allies.

But if the navy brass were not enamored of the appointment, almost everyone else in high military and political circles was. Canaris had the reputation of being a spy par excellence. He was also a devoted right-wing nationalist who had traveled all over the globe and demonstrated an uncanny ability to keep his footing in difficult situations. Indeed, the appointment seemed a fitting culmination to an eventful thirty-year career.

The son of a prosperous Ruhr industrialist whose ancestors had mi-

grated to Germany from northern Italy in the seventeenth century, Canaris joined the navy as an eighteen-year-old cadet in 1905. He spent several years aboard a cruiser in the South Atlantic and in the Caribbean, showing the German imperial flag and protecting Germany's commercial interests. A lover of foreign languages who already spoke English, passable French, and some Russian, Canaris took advantage of the Latin American cruise to become fluent in Spanish.

When World War I broke out, he was an officer on the light cruiser *Dresden*, one of the ships in Vice-Admiral Count Maximilian von Spee's squadron. On November 1, 1914, Spee's ships sank two British heavy cruisers off Valparaiso, Chile, in an action for which Canaris was decorated. But in December, the Royal Navy cornered Spee off the Falklands and sank every one of his ships except the *Dresden*, which managed to retreat into Chilean waters, where the crew scuttled it. Interned on Quiriquina Island, Canaris escaped to the mainland and trekked several hundred miles over the Andes on horseback into pro-German Argentina. Posing as an Anglo-Chilean named Reed Rosas, he acquired a passport in Buenos Aires and sailed home aboard an ocean liner belonging to the neutral Dutch.

Canaris's feat caught the eye of naval intelligence, and in November of 1915, he was dispatched to Spain on his first undercover mission: to arrange supply facilities for German U-boats. Ordered back to Germany in 1916 for sea duty, he was detained near the Swiss border by the Italians, who planned to hand him over to the French as a German spy. Faced with execution, Canaris somehow managed to escape.

According to one, perhaps fanciful, account, he lured a priest into his cell, strangled him, and then walked away, disguised in the holy man's cassock. Another rumor had him cajoling a Spanish ship captain into freeing him on the coast of Spain instead of delivering him to the French at Marseilles. In any case, in March 1916, Canaris surfaced in Madrid and that autumn made another daring escape. He sailed a small boat into the Mediterranean and rendezvoused with a U-boat, which spirited him away to Germany and a hero's welcome. Canaris's exploits earned him the Iron Cross, First Class—which paved the way for his first command. By the time Germany surrendered in 1918, he was a U-boat skipper with at least three kills to his credit.

Appalled by the postwar revolutionary chaos, Canaris threw himself into a variety of right-wing causes. He joined the Freikorps and, in 1919, served on the court-martial that exonerated the murderers of the Spartacist insurrectionists, Karl Liebknecht and Rosa Luxemburg. The following year, he was imprisoned briefly for supporting the failed putsch of Dr. Wolfgang Kapp against the Weimar Republic. In 1924, as one of a clique of officers

A Nazi battle flag flies above the Abwehr headquarters on Tirpitz-Ufer in Berlin's Tiergarten district. The spy agency's offices were actually down the street in town houses that connected internally to the main building.

working on clandestine naval rearmament, Canaris traveled to Osaka to scout prospects for a secret submarine-building program with the Japanese. The following year, he visited Madrid on a similar mission, renewing friendships with many of the men who were to become Spain's ruling elite a decade later under the Nationalist leader, Francisco Franco.

Canaris alternated undercover assignments with stretches at sea, but his political and diplomatic skills remained his strongest suit. "With the finest feel for foreign psychology and mentality, together with uncommon linguistic ability, he knows, in exemplary fashion, how to deal with foreigners (from the lowly to the prominent), whose trust he then soon possesses," wrote one superior in an evaluation. "If he were to have such a duty, there would be no obstacle for him; no area is so closed off that he would not get in and get to the person in question in order then in an amazingly short time to run the show, with a childish, innocent face." And now, as chief of the Abwehr, he had exactly such a duty.

Like many military men, Canaris welcomed the advent of Hitler. "Being a patriot," a friend recalled, "all he felt at first was the vitality that the National Socialist movement transmitted to the nation as a whole." But in accepting the Abwehr directorship, Canaris had struck a Faustian bargain. As the Nazi party and the German state grew increasingly inseparable, he came to realize that his beloved fatherland had fallen into the grip of evil forces, and for the next nine years he would balance on a knife edge, torn between cooperating with Hitler and trying to overthrow him. His dilemma prompted one observer to call him "the Hamlet of conservative Germany."

When Canaris moved into Patzig's former office, a high-ceilinged room with a small balcony overlooking the Landwehr Canal, he brought with him a few mementos from his long career, including a camp cot, a photograph of Francisco Franco with a lengthy personal dedication, a Japanese painting of the devil, an old, worn-out Persian carpet, a model of the *Dresden*, and a desk ornament from Japan—three bronze monkeys representing the saying see-no-evil, hear-no-evil, speak-no-evil. He covered one wall with a giant map of the world. On another, he hung an etching of Admiral Konstantínos Kanáris, the daring nineteenth-century hero of Greece's war of independence with Turkey. Although they were not related, he encouraged the rumor that the Greek admiral was a distant relative.

Despite their new boss's glamorous past and lofty reputation as a master spy, the staff's first impressions were less than overwhelming. "Compared with the brisk and energetic Captain Patzig," one of them noted, Canaris "seemed too old and spent for the job." Another wrote that he looked more like "the impresario of a music hall than a senior German officer." The

Abwehr veterans were also taken aback by Canaris's seemingly unabashed enthusiasm for the Nazis. Unlike his predecessor, who scarcely bothered to conceal his contempt for Hitler's minions, Canaris larded his speeches with party slogans and vows of loyalty. Being a true soldier and a National Socialist were one and the same, he said, since both honored "performance of duty, obedience, comradeship, and the acceptance of one's obligation to the national community."

Canaris's first order of business was to make peace with the SD chief, Heydrich, since Abwehr relations with the Gestapo and the SD were worsening daily. Senior Abwehr officials claimed that the Gestapo was monitoring their telephone conversations and that the SD was encouraging junior officers who were also Nazis to spy on their colleagues who were not members of the party. And Abwehr field agents complained of repeated intrusions onto their turf.

During Canaris's very first month in office, Heydrich extended his operations outside Germany in brutal fashion. A former Stuttgart radio executive, Rudolf Formis, had been beaming anti-Nazi broadcasts into Germany from Czechoslovakia. Heydrich assigned the job of suppressing Formis to a Nazi street brawler named Alfred Naujocks. Posing as a skier on holiday, Naujocks drove across the border from Dresden and found Formis in a country inn outside Prague. Heydrich wanted Formis brought back alive. But the kidnapping was bungled; in a struggle with Naujocks and another Gestapo agent, Formis was shot dead.

Canaris and Heydrich were old acquaintances from navy days. A dozen years earlier, Heydrich had been a young cadet serving under Canaris on the training cruiser *Berlin.* In addition, the two intelligence chiefs shared a mutual dislike of Admiral Raeder, whom Heydrich blamed for running him out of the service. With a promising career ahead of him, he had been forced to resign in a matter of honor involving a young woman whose father had high navy connections. Embittered and vengeful, Heydrich volunteered for the only uniformed service that would have him—Himmler's SS.

Heydrich professed to welcome Canaris's appointment. Soon thereafter, SS Lieut. Colonel Werner Best, the Gestapo's legal adviser, worked out a modus operandi for cooperation. It was agreed that the Abwehr would be responsible for all military espionage and counterespionage and that the Gestapo and the SD would confine themselves, in general, to political police work. Both sides pledged to jointly oppose any new intelligence unit that other organizations of the state might attempt to create. To seal the new spirit of cooperation, they agreed to hold regular meetings between department heads. Heydrich summoned his Gestapo bureau chiefs to Berlin and lectured them on the proper way to treat their Abwehr com-

rades, and Canaris, as a gesture of goodwill, agreed to cover the expenses of Heydrich's personnel "during surveillances wherever the Gestapo's budget and the SD organization are insufficient to cover them."

The two rivals took houses in the same leafy Berlin neighborhood near the Grünewald, and their lives soon became intertwined. There were Sunday afternoon croquet parties on the Canaris family's lawn and musical evenings in their home. Heydrich, an accomplished violinist, played Mozart with Canaris's wife, Erika, while Canaris, a gourmet cook, prepared his specialty—saddle of wild boar in a crust of black bread and red wine.

But beneath their amiable exteriors, both men remained wary and distrustful. Heydrich privately referred to the Abwehr chief as "that Levantine"

Wilhelm Canaris, head of the Abwehr *(second from left)*, and SD chief Reinhard Heydrich *(third from left)* sit side by side at a candlelight dinner for Wehrmacht and SS officers in 1935. Although the rival intelligence chiefs professed friendship for each other, they were mutually mistrustful.

and complained of his constant "snooping and nosing around." When Canaris hired an Algerian butler who reputedly spoke no German, Heydrich suspected that the man had been planted by the Abwehr to eavesdrop on conversations as he passed food and drink. Canaris, meanwhile, confidentially described Heydrich as a "brutal fanatic" and "the cleverest brute of them all."

From the beginning, Canaris concentrated on expanding his new empire. A dramatic shift in Germany's fortunes gave him an assist. In January 1935, Canaris's first month in office, Germany regained the coal-rich Saarland from France in a plebiscite sponsored by the League of Nations. Buoyed by the event, Hitler unveiled his theretofore secret program of rearmament. In March, he announced the existence of the Luftwaffe and proclaimed a military draft—all in defiance of the Versailles treaty. Hundreds of thousands of young men flocked to join the Wehrmacht, the new term used to describe the armed forces of the Third Reich. The rapid buildup of arms and manpower triggered a similar expansion in the intelligence agencies.

"With the introduction of universal military service," Canaris informed his staff, "we must allow for renewed and intensified action against the Wehrmacht and the German munitions industry by rival intelligence services." He rapidly enlarged the small bureau of 150 employees that he had inherited from Patzig into a far-reaching network capable of infiltrating not only Germany's European neighbors but also North and South America and the Middle East. Drawing heavily from the pool of former military officers but including some university professors and lawyers, he increased the staff to nearly 1,000 strong in just two years. (The total would peak, during the war, at 15,000.) In keeping with the Abwehr's expanded role, Canaris was promoted to admiral.

As Hitler waged his campaign to undo the restrictions of Versailles, he made special use of Canaris. In the winter of 1935-36, the Führer prepared for the risky reoccupation of the Rhineland—a gamble that he knew could trigger full-scale war. To help him gauge the odds, he looked to the little admiral for accurate appraisals of foreign reaction and dispatched him on secret missions abroad. During the four months prior to the successful Rhineland venture in March 1936, Canaris met with the Führer no fewer than seventeen times.

The admiral, in the meantime, left the day-to-day operation of the Abwehr in the hands of subordinates. In fact, the agency had always operated on the principle of decentralization. Although headquarters gave general instructions, it rarely exercised any direct control over agents. The core of the Abwehr remained the three original sections, or *Abteilungen*, set

up by Gempp in the 1920s. Section I, Secret Intelligence, gathered information about the economic and military strength of potential foreign enemies; Section II covered sabotage, subversion, psychological warfare, and the planning of commando operations; Section III handled counter-espionage and counterintelligence, including the infiltration of foreign intelligence services. There was also the Amtsgruppe Ausland, or foreign branch, which received reports from the Reich's military attachés abroad and evaluated military relations with other nations. Section Z, for Zentrale, or Central, took care of the agency's administrative and financial affairs.

Each section was divided into subunits according to specialty. Section I, for example, consisted of eleven subunits with expertise in such areas as air force technical intelligence, industrial intelligence, liaison with spy networks abroad, and had laboratories for producing invisible inks, false papers, and microphotography.

Attached to the Abteilungen were the *Abwehrstellen*, abbreviated to *Asts*, or outstations, each with its own assigned geographical region. The heads of the Asts operated semi-independently; although they took instructions from their section chiefs at the Tirpitz-Ufer headquarters, if they disagreed with an order they could appeal directly to Canaris. Each outstation chief also recruited and trained his own agents, called V-men (short for *Vertrauensmann*, or confidential agent).

Canaris directed each outstation to set up its own special team—a kind of spy ring within a spy ring. Insiders referred to these teams as *Hauskapellen*, a name referring to the court orchestras of the eighteenth-century German princes. A senior agent, called a *Kapellmeister*, or conductor, ran each "house orchestra."

The main tasks of the Hauskapellen were to uncover traitors within the Abwehr, infiltrate enemy intelligence services, and keep an eye out for foreigners who might be "turned" to Germany's advantage, either by re-cruiting them as spies or by feeding them *Spielmaterial*, or disinformation. The Hauskapellen engaged hundreds of informants, many of them waiters, busboys, chambermaids, bellhops, and bar hostesses at large hotels and popular nightspots. To oversee the entire operation, Canaris turned to an old Abwehr hand—Lieut. Commander Richard Protze of the navy, chief of Section III's counterespionage unit, IIIF. Known as Uncle Richard to his friends, Protze was the agent who had masterminded the breaking of the Sosnowski spy ring in 1934.

The SD was also growing. In June of 1936, Heinrich Himmler became chief of all German police, and with him rose Heydrich, who added chief of the Criminal Police to his portfolio. The elevation of Heydrich marked the end of the honeymoon period for Canaris. Heydrich angrily charged the

1 After popping a film cartridge into his Minox camera, a spy could shoot fifty black-and-white photographs.

2 To develop film, an agent loaded it into a lightproof tank and poured in small amounts of photographic chemicals. The logo on the tank's storage case features the manufacturer's initials, VEF, for Valsts Electro-Techniska Fabrika.

3 The 8-inch-high enlarger produced 2.5- x 3.5-inch prints. To the left are its power cord and transformer with switch. Negatives and prints were viewed through the hinged magnifying glass.

A Camera Tailor-Made for Espionage

When a manufacturer of electrical equipment in Riga, Latvia, introduced the Riga Minox to the world in 1937, it immediately became the camera of choice for German spies. Just over three inches long and weighing only 4.5 ounces, this tiny stainless-steel marvel was easy to conceal and simple to operate. Its lens, which could focus on items as close as eight inches, was ideal for photographing documents. It was equipped with a developing tank and a miniature enlarger, which agents operating in relatively safe surroundings used to process and print their film. Spies in hostile countries, however, found these accessories too cumbersome and incriminating, so they usually smuggled the undeveloped film back to Germany for processing.

Hauskapellen with performing unauthorized police functions, and Canaris retaliated by accusing the Gestapo of butting into IIIF's counterespionage cases before they were fully developed.

Again, Canaris attempted a negotiated settlement. He and the Gestapo's legal adviser, Colonel Best, got together once more and drafted a document called "Principles Governing Cooperation between the Gestapo and the Abwehr Offices of the Wehrmacht." The agreement, signed December 21, 1936, and promptly dubbed Treaty of the Ten Commandments, reasserted the Abwehr's primacy in counterespionage investigations and the Gestapo's primacy in police work. But too many details remained fuzzy. Heydrich was irritated by Canaris's flat refusal to disband the house orchestras. Canaris, on the other hand, chafed at the Gestapo's right, reaffirmed in the Ten Commandments, to investigate "culpable actions and the requisite follow-up operations."

Joseph Stalin *(top row, far left)*, standing with members of the Politburo, reviews the 1937 May Day parade in Red Square, shortly before launching a brutal purge of the military elite. Among those assassinated was Marshal Mikhail Tukhachevsky *(bottom row, far left)*, whom Reinhard Heydrich had implicated in a bogus anti-Stalin plot.

Hoping to forge closer ties, Canaris invited Heydrich to meet with him for early-morning horseback rides. Each day before work, the tall SD chieftain and the little Abwehr master spy, often joined by Best, could be seen trotting side by side in the Tiergarten, chatting amicably. But the friction between them remained.

The breach between Canaris and Heydrich widened in June of 1937 when the Soviet news agency Tass announced to the world that Mikhail Tukhachevsky, the Red Army's youngest marshal, had been executed, along with seven other top generals. Astonished, Canaris asked his own Russian experts for an explanation. They had none, but an Abwehr officer had heard a rumor at the War Ministry that the killings had been the result of an elaborate dirty trick engineered by Heydrich.

According to the story, Nikolai Skoblin, a former Russian White Army general working for the SD in Paris, had informed his handlers that a Russian opposition group led by Tukhachevsky was planning a coup against the Kremlin. The news gave Heydrich an idea: Why not turn the plot in Hitler's favor by forging documents that would make it appear that the Russian generals were conspiring with their German counterparts to kill Stalin? If the incriminating evidence fell into Soviet hands, the Nazis could sit back and watch the Red Army's leadership explode from within as Stalin exacted revenge on the traitors.

Heydrich brought in his jack-of-all-trades, Alfred Naujocks, who assembled a team of forgers. Using copies of old correspondence from the 1920s and early 1930s, when the Soviet and German armies enjoyed closer ties, the forgers went to work. In Zehlendorf, near Berlin, Naujocks discovered an engraver who could reproduce Russian signatures faultlessly. Soon, the SD had produced a thick dossier, including typed reports, complete with scribbled marginalia, telephone logs, and letters, all with seals, top-secret stamps, and other bureaucratic marks of authenticity. Then, to prepare the NKVD, the Soviet secret service, SD agents planted hints about the plot with sources who they knew would tell the Russians. Finally, the president of Czechoslovakia, Eduard Beneš, who was on good terms with Moscow, was made the dupe. He was persuaded to tell the Soviets about the dossier and inform them that they could have it for the right sum. The unsuspecting Czech played his role perfectly, and in May 1937, Heydrich had the satisfaction of seeing NKVD agents arrive in Berlin to conclude the deal.

The aftermath was the bloodiest purge in Red Army history. The killing of Tukhachevsky and the seven generals was only the beginning. In due course, seven of the nine judges who presided at the trial were also executed. By the time the bloodbath was over, Stalin's victims numbered more than 30,000. They included three out of the Red Army's five marshals,

eleven deputy defense commissars, and seventy-five of eighty members of the Supreme War Council.

Canaris, who regarded Stalin as the world's great menace, confronted his rival. "Why in heaven's name did you play such a game?" he asked. "The idea came from the Führer himself," Heydrich coldly replied. "The Russian armed forces had to be decimated at the top and weakened in consequence. The whole thing is a gambit on the Führer's part—it fits into his overall plan for the next few years."

The SD's blatant intrusion onto the Abwehr's foreign intelligence turf, and in such an unscrupulous manner, shook Canaris. For the first time, he began to question Hitler's qualifications to lead Germany. He never learned that the last laugh belonged to the Soviets. The SD documents were never introduced at Tukhachevsky's trial. Since the war, in fact, evidence has surfaced indicating that Stalin had planned to liquidate his generals months before Heydrich conceived his scheme and had begun moving against Tukhachevsky before he received the forgeries. Skoblin was actually a double agent working for the the NKVD, and it was thus Heydrich who played the fool. According to Walter Schellenberg, a young lawyer who was part of the SD brain trust, the three million rubles paid by the Soviets were themselves forgeries and specially marked. Every time an SD agent used one in Russia he was arrested.

Soon Canaris was hearing of other SD outrages. It was small wonder, considering the agency's mushrooming growth. By 1937, Heydrich's Berlin headquarters staff numbered several thousand, and they supported no fewer than 50,000 informants and agents in the field, most of them untrained and hired solely for the purity of their Nazi ideology. The SD information bureau, for example, insisted that Tukhachevsky had belonged to a "Western-Jewish-Freemason" clique struggling for power in the Soviet Union. When Canaris claimed that SD amateurishness was disrupting the Abwehr's work, Heydrich brushed his complaints aside.

Shortly after the Tukhachevsky affair, Canaris bumped into Konrad Patzig, his Abwehr predecessor, and complained bitterly of Heydrich and his Nazi colleagues. "At the very outset of our conversation," Patzig recalled, "he told me they were all criminals from top to bottom, and bent on ruining Germany." But when Patzig suggested that he resign in protest, Canaris replied, "If I go, Heydrich takes over, and that'll be the end of everything."

In early 1938, Canaris made one great push to gain the upper hand over his archrival. His effort came in response to a piece of SD skulduggery designed to rid Hitler of two top military officials who were resisting the Führer's plans for foreign expansion. One of the disfavored was the war minister, Field Marshal Werner von Blomberg, who had recently married

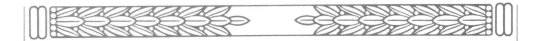

SD agent Alfred Naujocks *(left)* takes an order from his boss, SS-Brigadeführer Reinhard Heydrich. As a charter member of the SD, Naujocks was entrusted with many of Heydrich's most unsavory missions, including those involving kidnapping and murder.

a government secretary in a ceremony attended by Hitler. Heydrich's Criminal Police investigated the bride's background, discovered that she was a former prostitute, and assembled a collection of pornographic photographs of her. Presented with the evidence, Hitler forced Blomberg to resign. The other intended SD victim was the commander in chief of the army, General Werner von Fritsch. To topple Fritsch, Heydrich's investigators produced a convicted thief, one Otto Schmidt, who claimed to have been a witness to a homosexual liaison involving the general. Fritsch, too, was fired, but he refused to leave quietly, demanding that a court-martial try the charge against him.

The scandal appalled Canaris, for he and the two victims were kindred spirits who shared the fear that Hitler was leading Germany headlong into a war for which the nation was ill-prepared. Canaris concluded that

Blomberg's case was a *fait accompli* and that it would be useless to intervene, but he ordered his men to launch their own investigation into the charges against Fritsch. They soon discovered the truth—the man whom Otto Schmidt had seen with a male prostitute was not the army commander in chief Fritsch, but a retired captain who spelled his name *Frisch*. The captain readily confessed to the sexual encounter.

Learning that the Abwehr had spoiled their case, the Gestapo determined to prevent Captain Frisch from testifying by arresting him themselves. But Canaris was one step ahead of them. He had his ace counterespionage man Richard Protze post an Abwehr photographer near Frisch's apartment to photograph the Gestapo agents as they whisked away the star witness. The photograph saved the life of Captain Frisch and the reputation of General Fritsch.

Determined, as Canaris put it, to release "the Wehrmacht from a Cheka nightmare" (his sarcastic analogy between the Gestapo and the Soviet secret police), he rather naively drafted a proposal to the new army commander in chief, General Walther von Brauchitsch, demanding a thorough housecleaning of the SS leadership, starting at the top with Himmler and Heydrich. "As things stand," he wrote, "the continuance of fruitful cooperation by the Wehrmacht with responsible and senior members of the Gestapo involved in the defamation of General Fritsch, and thus in a malicious and insulting attack on the army, cannot be countenanced." But his efforts went for nought. The generals were not prepared to avenge General Fritsch, their former chief, especially after Hitler formally rehabilitated him and gave him a regiment to command. And any misgivings they might have had were soon lost in the national euphoria that greeted the union with Austria, which occurred in the middle of the Fritsch trial.

As Hitler sent his troops into Austria in March 1938, Canaris made sure his agents rushed to Vienna to prevent the Austrian military intelligence files from falling into the hands of the SD. The Abwehr agents succeeded, and Canaris turned the information over to Protze for action by his Hauskapellen. But in the struggle for ascendancy, the Abwehr was losing. As the Nazi party succeeded in taking over the German state, Heydrich operated from an ever-stronger political base. Heydrich also had another advantage: Unlike Canaris, he was a skilled bureaucrat. Whereas Canaris despised organizational duties and desk work, Heydrich loved them. He enjoyed driving his men mercilessly, barking orders in a high-pitched staccato. And he would stoop to anything.

According to Walter Schellenberg, Heydrich's compulsion was "always to know more than others, to know everything about everyone, whether it touched on the political, professional, or most intimate personal aspects

Salon Kitty, a swanky bordello in Berlin, was secretly run by the SD to eavesdrop on a clientele of foreign diplomats and high government officials. Double walls in each room concealed wires that ran from hidden microphones to recording equipment in the basement.

of their lives, and to use this knowledge to render them completely dependent on him."

As one means to this end, Heydrich opened an SD brothel in one of Berlin's most expensive residential districts. The brothel, called Salon Kitty, catered to German civil servants, foreign diplomats, and businessmen. Each of the nine bedrooms was rigged with concealed microphones wired to recording equipment in the basement. A notorious womanizer, Heydrich became a regular patron himself. The lechery of the SD chief provided the setting for what was perhaps the only practical joke that an underling ever tried to play on him.

Whenever Heydrich showed up for an "inspection tour" of Salon Kitty, his standing orders were for all the microphones to be turned off. But on one occasion, the rough-and-ready Naujocks decided to have some fun: He recorded Heydrich's visit. Naujocks then thought better of the prank and erased the tapes. But Heydrich had spies, even in Salon Kitty. The following day, he summoned Naujocks to his office. "If you think you can make fun of me, Naujocks, think again," Heydrich told him. "Get out." Naujocks never tested Heydrich's sense of humor again.

In contrast to the obsessive Heydrich, Canaris was a careless administrator. He delegated day-to-day operations to his section chiefs, and as a result the Abwehr, which was already highly decentralized, sprawled beyond his control. Canaris preferred to spend his time practicing what he called intelligence politics—that is, making use of secret Abwehr data to quietly influence the political and military policies of the Third Reich. And at this he was a master. At the onset of the Spanish Civil War in July of 1936, for example, he became instrumental in committing Germany military aid

to Francisco Franco's Nationalists. The German Foreign Office was appalled at the implications of such intervention. But in the end, Hitler gave the Spanish envoys the promises they sought, and a contingent of German warplanes, followed by Luftwaffe officers in civilian clothes, was soon en route to Spain. When Admiral Canaris flew to Salamanca in October of 1936 to meet with Franco, the spy master and the leader of the Spanish rebellion embraced warmly.

Canaris also loved traveling, especially in southern Europe. He spent nearly as much time in the field as in the office and sometimes assigned himself minor intelligence assignments that properly should have been given to a low-level agent. Once, driving back from Spain, a blizzard forced him to stop and seek refuge. As the staff at the Tirpitz-Ufer headquarters frantically scoured the countryside for their lost boss, Canaris passed the time happily in a farmhouse, having persuaded a peasant family to take him in. When Heydrich heard about the incident, he sneered, "Is that how they run the Abwehr?" In fact, it was.

"His tours of inspection came to be dreaded by his subordinates," recalled Wilhelm Hoettl, an Austrian Abwehr agent who later worked for the SD. "He was wont to turn everything completely topsy-turvy and to leave a chaotic mess in his wake. His sectional chiefs, aware of this idiosyncrasy, made it a rule to send an officer close on the admiral's heels with orders to tidy up the mess and put everything in order again, regardless of any instructions or directives the admiral might have given. This could be done without undue risk, for Canaris never bothered to find out whether his instructions had been obeyed."

Canaris had other peculiarities that made working with him difficult. He was moody and a famous hypochondriac, inordinately afraid of germs. To sneeze in his presence was to risk banishment. He could be brusque and impatient in conversation, chopping at subordinates with the command "Kürzer! Kürzer!" (Make it snappy!) He also hated military trappings and rarely wore his own medals. According to Hoettl, "The sight of a decoration immediately evoked his resentment, and any officer who appeared before him wearing the ribbon of the Knight's Cross could be quite sure that his proposals were already as good as rejected."

But perhaps the Abwehr chief's most noted quirk was his obsession with animals, especially his two pet dachshunds, Seppel and Sabine, who accompanied him everywhere, riding in his Mercedes limousine and trailing him about the office. Canaris talked to them constantly and was convinced that a man who did not like dogs could not be trusted. This attitude mystified his Section II chief, Colonel Erwin Lahousen, who wrote, "Canaris was the most difficult superior I came up against in my thirty-year career.

A Nazi Enclave in the United States

American Nazis march into Madison Square Garden while outside the arena (inset), curious bystanders gather.

Abwehr attempts to establish a fifth column in America were hindered rather than helped in 1936 when a clamorous convention of Nazi supporters in Buffalo voted to form the German-American Bund. Even after Hitler disavowed the group in 1938 because of the public outcry ignited by their paramilitary training camps and anti-Jewish newspa-

pers, the Bundists refused to disband. On February 20, 1939, in New York's Madison Square Garden, they staged an emotionally charged Washington's Birthday celebration and pro-American rally, complete with goose-stepping storm troopers and stiff-armed salutes.

The cavernous arena rocked with cheers as the heavyset Bundesfüh-

rer Fritz Kuhn took the podium to call for a "socially just, white gentile-ruled United States." Later that same year, Kuhn was revealed to be a racketeer as well as an ideologue when a jury indicted him on charges of embezzling Bund funds. The organization dissolved soon thereafter without ever having posed any real threat to United States security.

Some 22,000 people pack the sports arena, which has been bedecked with a thirty-foot-tall George Washington banner and Nazi and American flags (*right*). Many spectators were not Bundists, but rather anti-Nazis curious to see what the movement was all about. Despite the Garden's ban on anti-Semitic rhetoric, Fritz Kuhn (*below*) delivers an attack on Jews under a banner that proclaims, "Stop Jewish domination of Christian America." Kuhn's tirade was interrupted by Isadore Greenbaum, a Jewish plumber's assistant who rushed the rostrum shouting "Down with Hitler!" and received a pummeling in response (*inset, right*).

Having lost his pants in a one-sided fight with Nazi toughs, Isadore Greenbaum is arrested for disturbing the peace *(left)*. He was released from jail the next day after friends paid his $25 fine. Elsewhere outside the Garden, mounted policemen control an angry mob of demonstrators brandishing antifascist signs *(below)*.

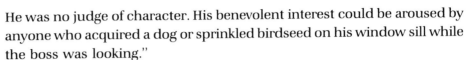

He was no judge of character. His benevolent interest could be aroused by anyone who acquired a dog or sprinkled birdseed on his window sill while the boss was looking."

Canaris's behavior also amazed Hoettl, who observed that he seemed unconscious of any need for human affection, so much did he worship his dogs. "The admiral's dachshunds were the terror of his entourage," Hoettl wrote. "Their state of health was his greatest concern, and they meant much more to him at all times than any human being; a minor indisposition on the part of one of his beloved pets caused him to suffer from the most acute depression and seriously affected the efficiency of his work.

"Wherever he was, in Germany or abroad, he invariably telephoned each day to ask about the dogs, demanding to know the minutest details of their menus and their natural functions; on one occasion, the chief of the Spanish secret police received the surprise of his life when a recording of a telephone call that the admiral had made from Tangiers to Berlin was placed before him. He had hoped to gather some interesting tidbits of political information; instead he received a detailed report on the natural functions of an ailing dachshund!"

Regardless of the boss's idiosyncrasies, the Abwehr was chalking up successes. More than 250 agents were in place in Great Britain, including several domestics working in the homes of key British officials. By August 1938, Canaris could claim that most British airfields had been mapped, as well as coastal installations, including the oil-storage depots between London and the North Sea port of Hull.

The Abwehr also managed to penetrate the Continental operations of MI-6, Britain's secret service. Knowing that The Hague was a hub of MI-6 activity, Canaris assigned his Hauskapellen master Richard Protze to Holland to uncover British clandestine activity and ferret out British spies. Protze, after feigning his own retirement from the navy, moved with his former Abwehr secretary and mistress to a village in the Dutch countryside. It was not long before he made contact with a Dutchman working part-time as a shadow for the British secret service and turned the man simply by offering him more money than the British were paying. Through this double agent, Protze uncovered other British intelligence sources, among them a German diplomat about to defect. In July 1939, the trail led to a man the British referred to as Dr. K—their naval superspy who reported to contacts in The Hague. Dr. K, whose real name was Otto Krueger, was a prosperous and respected German engineer who did consulting work for the Kriegsmarine in the shipyards at Kiel. Recruited by the British after the First World War, Krueger had been passing the most sensitive German naval secrets—many of which were his own inventions—to his handlers for two decades. His arrest marked the demise of the British spy network operating out of Holland.

The United States was another prime target. It was clear to Canaris that American industrial know-how (which, Hitler was convinced, was entirely the creation of immigrant German engineers) would be the "decisive factor" in any future global conflict. Canaris hoped to find a receptive audience in the United States, where there were some voices raised for Hitler. The German-American Bund, vociferously pro-Nazi and anti-Semitic, had thousands of members scattered throughout the country and staged occasional rallies in places such as Madison Square Garden. But Bund membership represented only a tiny fraction of the millions of Americans of German descent, and the Abwehr found few among them who were willing to betray their American homeland. Canaris had to build his American network with a nucleus of spies sent from Germany.

As early as 1927, the Abwehr had dispatched its first agent, an aeronautical engineer named Wilhelm Lonkowski, across the Atlantic. Working under the alias William Schneider, Lonkowski settled in Hoboken, New Jersey, and found employment with the Ireland Aircraft Corporation on Long Island. Two more German agents, Werner Gudenberg and Otto Voss, soon joined him at the plant. Later on, Lonkowski became the United States correspondent for the German aviation magazine *Luftreise* (Air travel)—the perfect cover for someone in search of technical data. He then merged his operation with that of Ignatz Theodor Griebl, a Bavarian-born physician who was practicing medicine on Manhattan's Upper East Side in the heavily German Yorkville district.

To act as a courier for Lonkowski and Griebl, the Abwehr recruited a steward on the ocean liner *Bremen*, and soon American military data was flowing smoothly and swiftly from New York Harbor to the port of Bremerhaven. On one occasion, barely three weeks elapsed between a request for the plans of a new Sikorsky aircraft pontoon and their delivery to Germany. The operation also provided metallurgical data, aircraft specifications from Boeing, Douglas, and Vought, blueprints for destroyers, and the results of tactical air exercises by the United States Army Air Corps.

The spy ring continued to function even after 1935, when Lonkowski was uncovered by a customs officer as he attempted to pass a collection of drawings of aircraft and a filmstrip of aviation details to an Abwehr courier on the New York docks. Lonkowski managed to escape to Canada and get away on a German freighter sailing down the St. Lawrence.

One secret that particularly interested the Germans involved a sophisticated bombsight, developed by Carl T. Norden in his New York City plant, that provided for the automatic aiming and release of bombloads. The

Having just disembarked from the liner *Bremen*, Nikolaus Ritter *(left)*, director of the air intelligence section of the Abwehr's Hamburg station, arrives at Pier 86 in Manhattan on a mission to steal the blueprints to an American bombsight. The photo was taken by a dock photographer employed by the FBI before Ritter was identified as a spy.

Lonkowski-Griebl ring had no access to the bombsight. But in September 1937, the Abwehr's Hamburg station received, out of the blue, two drawings of a section of the bombsight. A note accompanying them claimed that more documents were available if the Abwehr would send someone to New York to get them.

The Hamburg station's new air intelligence chief, Major Nikolaus Ritter, a former United States resident who had recently returned to Germany after losing his job as a director of an American textile company, wanted to undertake the task himself. Canaris objected on the grounds that should Ritter be exposed, the Abwehr's entire American operation would be compromised. But he relented, and Ritter sailed for New York.

Twice Ritter had close calls, once aboard ship when he ran into an old New York acquaintance, and again when the special cane umbrella he carried, with a hollow shaft, caught the attention of a customs officer. "Real spy stuff," the official laughed; Ritter laughed with him.

Ritter found his contact in Brooklyn, who directed him to the possessor of the bombsight secrets, Hermann Lang. Lang was a machinist and draftsman who had been born in Germany but was now a United States citizen. Married with a daughter, he lived a suburban Long Island life and commuted daily to the Norden plant in lower Manhattan. There, as an inspector, he handed out blueprints to various working groups each day,

The German radio station at Gleiwitz *(below)*, on the Polish border, was the target of a phony SD raid designed to implicate Poles in an act of aggression. The morning after the attack, the front page of a Berlin newspaper featured the headline, "Bold attack on Radio Gleiwitz, Polish raiders cross the border, bloody fighting with German police."

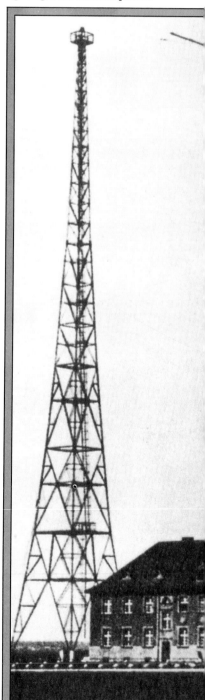

taking them back for safekeeping each night. Some nights he took certain blueprints home, made copies of them on tracing paper, and secretly returned them the next morning. Now Lang handed over copies to Ritter. They fitted comfortably into the shaft of Ritter's umbrella, which a steward aboard the *Bremen* then carried back to Germany in October 1937.

Although German engineers were unable to extrapolate the missing segments of the bombsight from the partial blueprints, there was enough data to help in the development of the Luftwaffe's own version, called *Adler-Gerät* (eagle apparatus). In early 1938, the Abwehr brought Lang to Germany so that Hermann Göring could thank him personally.

Whatever his successes in the field, Canaris was plagued more and more often by doubts about Germany's leadership and the path down which the nation was headed. In March of 1939, Canaris happened to be in Hitler's office at the chancellery when news arrived that the British had issued a formal guarantee of support to Poland. Livid with rage, the Führer strode back and forth, pounding the table with his fists and swearing to fix his enemies "a devil's brew." Canaris, who had never seen Hitler lose control this way, returned to his own headquarters a shaken man. "I've seen a madman," he confided to an aide. "I still can't take it in. He's mad, mad, do you understand? Mad!"

Nonetheless, the following month, Canaris began to prepare the Abwehr for its role in the surprise invasion of Poland. Colonel Hans Piekenbrock's Section I would scout the location of the Polish forces and report on their strength and objectives, assisted by a squadron of high-altitude spy planes. Lahousen's Section II began assembling commando teams, largely from the outstations in Königsberg and Breslau. Their job was to prevent the Poles from sabotaging their own industrial centers and lines of communication to thwart the Germans. The main targets to be seized were the bridge over the Vistula at Dirschau south of Danzig and the railroad tunnel at Jablunkov Pass in the Beskids along the Czechoslovakian border, which carried all train traffic between eastern Germany, southern Poland, and the Balkans. Dressed in civilian clothes, the commandos would slip into Poland and be ready for action before the first shot was fired. But even as he prepared for war, Canaris tried to forestall it. He circulated situation reports playing up British determination to support Poland and had his foreign branch publish a document obliquely criticizing Hitler's brash course.

Late in July, while in the middle of his planning, Canaris received a disconcerting visit from the head of the SD's foreign intelligence section, who informed him that Hitler wanted the Abwehr to help Heydrich carry out a special operation. The Abwehr was to provide 150 Polish army

uniforms, weapons, and pay books, as well as 364 of Canaris's own men.

The operation would involve simulated attacks by SD men, dressed as Poles and speaking Polish, on a number of German border installations, including the radio station at Gleiwitz in Upper Silesia. Heydrich's trusty henchman, Alfred Naujocks, was in charge of the charade at the radio station. The plan called for his pseudo-Poles to exchange blank shots with SD men dressed in German frontier-guard uniforms, then take over the radio station and break into the evening broadcast with anti-German propaganda.

In his instructions to Naujocks, Heydrich wrote: "Actual proof of Polish attacks is essential both for the foreign press and for German propaganda." Authentic casualties were essential. The planners decided that concentration-camp inmates with Slavic features would be brought to the scene and murdered. The code word for the phony attacks would be "Grandma's dead."

On August 25, Hitler issued orders for the Wehrmacht to begin the invasion of Poland the next morning. The Abwehr's sabotage and combat teams and the SD provocateurs prepared for action. Then, Hitler abruptly canceled the operation. Upon learning that the Italians would not support him and that Britain and Poland had signed a long-term military pact, the Führer briefly lost his nerve. A few days later, however, he regained it, and the phony Polish assault went on as planned.

On August 31, Naujocks and his men charged into the Gleiwitz radio station—and could not find the right switches to pull to get on the air. After a few frantic moments, they discovered an emergency microphone used to issue storm warnings. The proper sound effects, including a statement in Polish condemning Germany, went out to the station's listeners. The SD gang then fled, leaving behind a body as proof of Polish aggression. The next morning, the Nazi-controlled press trumpeted news of Polish provocation. In the Reichstag, Hitler brazenly declared that besides the incident at Gleiwitz, there had been thirteen other border violations.

That same afternoon, in the dimly lit corridors of the Abwehr headquarters, Canaris drew aside a trusted colleague and whispered, "This means the end of Germany." But the next morning, September 1, 1939, faced once again with his crisis of allegiance, he delivered a pep talk to his top aides, urging each of them to pledge unconditional loyalty to the Führer. He ended the meeting with a loud "Heil Hitler!" ✚

Under Cover in New York

During the 1930s and early 1940s, scores of Abwehr agents called New York City home. Like other foreign visitors in the days before transatlantic air travel, the German spies arrived on ocean liners that docked at the Port of New York, the nation's largest and busiest harbor. Many of the agents saw no need to travel farther afield to ply their craft; the New York waterfront was a treasure-trove of information useful to a foreign agent. From New York's 1,800 piers and wharves, hundreds of thousands of tons of goods and matériel, including motor vehicles, copper, iron, and steel, were shipped annually to countries such as France and England. Facts about cargoes, shipping schedules, and sailing routes proved invaluable to German naval intelligence, particularly in deploying U-boats in the North Atlantic. A German agent could often determine the nature of a ship's cargo simply by strolling up to its berth and reading the markings on crates stacked on the dock for loading. A friendly chat with a seaman in a local bar could reveal the ship's destination and departure date.

In a city with 600,000 German-Americans as of 1940, Hitler's spies moved about easily and undetected. The German-American community of Yorkville on Manhattan's Upper East Side not only provided ideal cover but also served as a hunting ground for new recruits to spy for Germany. Abwehr agents solicited help from German-American supervisors, engineers, metallurgists, and others assigned to top-secret projects inside New York's defense plants. Most of these workers were naturalized Americans who were appalled by the suggestion that they betray their adopted country. Others, however, desperate for cash or fearing reprisals against relatives in Germany, cooperated, providing their Nazi benefactors with everything from samples of cable being installed in navy ships to drawings of destroyers.

Two unfortunate German agents (*inset*) arrested in New York City in 1938 arrive at federal court. Most German agents sent to America landed at New York's

Dr. Ignatz Griebl offered his services as a spy in a 1934 letter to Propaganda Minister Joseph Goebbels. Griebl's network became one of the biggest New York-based spy rings.

A Haven for Spies in Yorkville

In 1934, Dr. Ignatz Griebl, a prominent Yorkville physician and political leader, started a spy ring whose ranks eventually included agents at defense installations as far away as Boston, Buffalo, Baltimore, and Newport News, Virginia.

Although he was an outspoken supporter of the Third Reich and boldly displayed a Nazi flag at his speaking engagements, Griebl's reputation as a surgeon and an obstetrician shielded him from government scrutiny. In late 1934, Griebl merged his ring with that of fellow spy Wilhelm Lonkowski. After his partner returned to Germany in 1935, Griebl ran the operation, meeting with his agents in the German beer halls and restaurants of Yorkville.

Before joining Griebl's ring, ex-United States Army sergeant Guenther Rumrich offered his skills to the publishers of the Nazi newspaper, *Völkischer Beobachter* (National observer).

◁ Katherine Moog Busch *(left)*, a socialite and mistress of Ignatz Griebl, chats with her attorney in 1938. When she and Griebl visited Berlin in 1937, the Abwehr suggested she open a brothel in Washington, D.C., to prey on government officials.

Yorkville's nightspots glow in a jumble of neon along East 86th Street. Rudi's and Maxl's *(background)* was a favorite spy hangout.

A member of Ritter's espionage ring, Frederick Duquesne, a native South African, had spied for Germany in England during World War I. In the United States, he posed as a lecturer, writer, and botanist.

Lilly Stein was an artist's model who lived stylishly on Manhattan's East Side and hobnobbed with the elite of New York and Washington. Her influential and garrulous boyfriends, including a high-ranking Foreign Service officer, were wellsprings of information that proved invaluable to Ritter and Duquesne.

New York's Hotel Taft was known as the Abwehr hotel because of its popularity with German spies. Nikolaus Ritter made the Taft his headquarters when he organized a spy ring in 1937.

The Purloined Blueprints

In October 1937, Major Nikolaus Ritter of the Abwehr arrived in New York to establish a spy ring that would specialize in stealing aviation secrets. He soon arranged to meet with Hermann Lang, a plant inspector for Norden, a company that made a new, top-secret bombsight for warplanes. In an apartment in Brooklyn, Lang handed over drawings of the device that he had purloined from the company. Sent back to Germany, those drawings helped the Luftwaffe perfect its own bombsight. Lang's reward for his skulduggery was a trip to Berlin at the Abwehr's expense.

German-born Hermann Lang *(top)* stole blueprints of the Norden bombsight *(above)* from a Manhattan defense plant. He told Nikolaus Ritter that he wanted no money for his action but merely wished to help Germany.

peline
ermany

ealing documents and data,
spies confronted the prob-
sneaking their plunder to
ny. During the 1930s, crew
rs on ships of the North Ger-
oyd and Hamburg-America
ted as couriers for the spies.
war broke out in 1939 and
ships were unwelcome in
an waters, the agents turned
American Airlines' Clipper
between New York and Lis-
even more efficient means
hing Abwehr headquarters
shortwave radio.

A Pan American Clipper, the "flying boat," takes off from Bowery Bay near La Guardia Airport. René Mezenen *(inset)*, a flight steward on the Clipper, smuggled secrets for the Ritter-Duquesne ring.

Johanna Hofmann, a hairdresser on the German liner *Europa*, carried packages and messages to and from Germany for Guenther Rumrich. Some crew members of the *Bremen* *(opposite, top)*, the flagship of the North German Lloyd Line, also worked as spy-ring couriers.

Josef Klein, a commercial photographer and amateur radio operator, poses in his New York apartment with his German shepherd and a shortwave transmitter he built for the Abwehr in 1940

(3) My honor is your house as long as you feel like staying. I've got a number of good connections and am almost 100% sure that I can get you a decent job that will make you forget all about the army.

You say you'll be in New York by June. That would coincide with my vacation. Let me know by which boat you are arriving and I'll meet you at the Army Base.

Don't let the tropics get you in the mean-time, old topper; take it by remembering that there are other things in life besides reveille, drill, retreat, parade and paydays. If this sounds like a preaching sermon to you, ok, then it is one.

After Guenther Rumrich's arrest, an FBI search of his apartment *(left)* turned up a letter from Rumrich inviting an Army buddy, Erich Glaser, to become a spy. Glaser was also arrested.

The Collapse of a Network

The arrest of Guenther Rumrich in 1938 led to the downfall of the Griebl-Lonkowski network. Investigators cracked the larger Ritter-Duquesne ring by enlisting the help of a German-American machinist, William Sebold, who claimed in 1939 that Abwehr agents had asked him to be a courier. The FBI set up a phony business for Sebold and, through a two-way mirror, recorded scores of spies passing information to him. After two years, the FBI had 20,000 feet of film and an airtight case against Ritter's men.

A police official examines part of the small arsenal seized by the Federal Bureau of Investigation from the home of Everett Roeder, an engineer who worked for Sperry Gyroscope on Long Island and spied for Frederick Duquesne (opposite).

Double agent William Sebold used an office in the Knicker-bocker Building (above) as a spy trap. Photos (right) taken through a two-way mirror show several spies, among them Hermann Lang (top) and Frederick Duquesne (second from top), giving Sebold (back to camera) information for Germany.

A handcuffed Felix Jahnke *(top)*, radio operator for the Ritter-Duquesne ring, is hustled into Brooklyn's federal court in 1941. Everett Roeder *(above)* got a sixteen-year sentence for his work with Duquesne. Johanna Hofmann *(right)*, betrayed by Guenther Rumrich, received a four-year prison term in 1938 for her association with Ignatz Griebl. The federal government subpoenaed Griebl's wife, Maria *(top right)*, as a witness.

Reckonings in the Courts of Law

The FBI's carefully accumulated evidence toppled two of Nazi Germany's largest spy networks. On October 14, 1938, the trial of eighteen operatives of the Griebl-Lonkowski ring began at the federal courthouse in Manhattan. Only four of the spies were actually in custody, however. Fourteen, including the group's two masterminds, had managed to flee the country earlier and had to be tried *in absentia*. All were convicted of conspiring to steal United States military secrets; the four who remained were sentenced to an average of four years in prison. Because he cooperated with the government, Guenther Rumrich received only a two-year sentence. Despite the fact that most of the ring had escaped punishment, United States Attorney Lamar Hardy claimed to be satisfied with the outcome, announcing that it served "as a warning to any nation engaged in or contemplating such activities in the United States."

In July 1941, an FBI dragnet swept up thirty-three members of the Ritter-Duquesne ring. Fourteen pleaded guilty immediately to various charges; nineteen were tried in September in Brooklyn. After weeks of testimony, the jury found all of the defendants guilty. Duquesne and Hermann Lang each received eighteen-year sentences; but Ritter, who had returned to Germany in 1937, was never punished.

Although these trials marked the end of the big networks, German agents in America continued to work either alone or in small groups throughout the war.

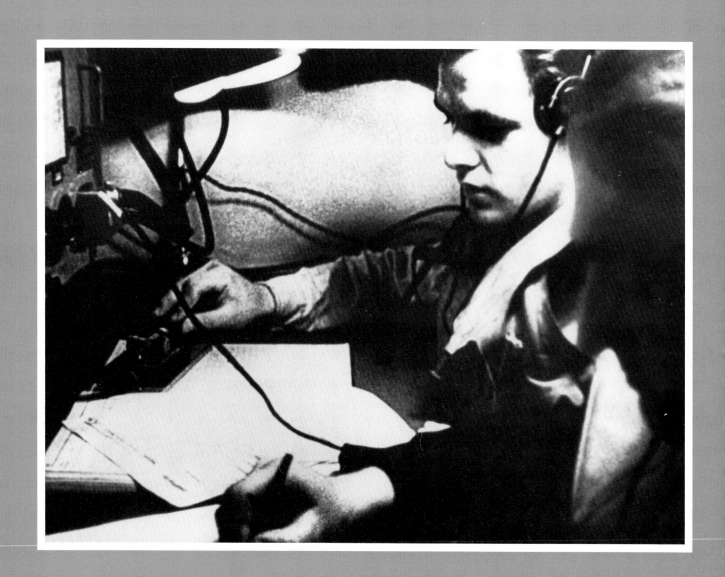

Agents for All Continents

he night of June 12, 1942, a German submarine, U-202, churned south-westward from the direction of Newfoundland toward the tip of Long Island. Hidden by a dense fog, the U-boat ran on the surface until within a mile or two of the coast, then submerged and lay on the bottom in about 100 feet of water. Around midnight it resurfaced, and a group of men emerged on the wet, slippery deck. All were wearing Kriegsmarine uniforms, but four of them were not sailors. They were something else entirely—Abwehr saboteurs. The uniforms were strictly a precaution: If captured upon landing, the saboteurs hoped to pass themselves off as regular combatants so that the Americans would send them to a POW camp rather than to the electric chair, the gas chamber, or the gallows.

As U-202 edged slowly through the darkness toward the Long Island shoreline, more than 1,000 miles to the south a second submarine, U-201, was approaching Ponta Vedra Beach, Florida, south of Jacksonville, with another four-man team. The two groups had been handpicked in Berlin to carry out Operation Pastorius—one of the boldest sabotage missions in the history of modern warfare.

Hitler's armed forces high command (OKW) had long considered the United States a sleeping giant. After President Franklin D. Roosevelt declared war on Germany, OKW officials began badgering the Abwehr chief, Admiral Wilhelm Canaris, to devise a plan to cripple American industry before the Americans could harness its gigantic potential.

Canaris assigned the task to one of his American specialists, a beefy, bull-necked agent named Walther Kappe. Before returning to his native Germany in 1937, Kappe had been active in promoting Nazi propaganda in Illinois and New York. Once his Pastorius teams had successfully infiltrated the United States, Kappe planned to slip back himself and run the operation from his adopted hometown of Chicago, communicating with his agents through coded advertisements in the *Chicago Tribune*. Targets included the Aluminum Company of America factories in East St. Louis, Illinois, Alcoa, Tennessee, and Massena, New York; the hydroelectric plants at Niagara Falls; the locks on the Ohio River between Louisville and Pitts-

Under the vigilant eye of a British intelligence officer (*right foreground*), **captured German agent Wolf Schmidt sends a deceptive radio message back to the Abwehr. The British caught dozens of spies during the war, most of whom chose to work for their captors rather than face execution for espionage.**

| Ernest Burger | George Dasch | Werner Thiel | Edward Kerling |

burgh; the Newark, New Jersey, railroad station; and the water system supplying New York City from nearby Westchester County.

All eight of Kappe's men, like him, had lived for years in the United States, spoke fluent English, and were well versed in American customs. Two were United States citizens, and one had a wife living in New York City. Kappe put the men through eight weeks of training at Quentz Lake, a forested estate outside Berlin. The program included instruction in hand-to-hand combat, techniques for making invisible ink, the use of various explosive devices, and mock attacks against German targets, including the Berlin railroad yard. Each man was given a set of forged American papers, including a birth certificate, draft deferment card, driver's license, and social security card. The men memorized bogus life stories and swore an oath to kill any member of the group who lost his resolve.

In late May 1942, the saboteurs arrived at the U-boat base at Lorient, France, to begin the 3,000-mile trip across the Atlantic. The team leaders carried $70,000 in cash to pay bribes and general expenses. Each team member received a money belt containing $4,000 and a billfold filled with $400 in small denominations.

When U-202 reached shallow water, the four agents slipped over the side into a rubber dinghy. They brought with them two shovels, a duffel bag filled with clothing, and four waterproof containers packed with ingenious explosive devices: dynamite disguised as lumps of coal and wooden blocks, TNT packed in wood shavings, incendiary bombs disguised as fountain

Eight German saboteurs stand for their FBI photographs in June 1942. In an undertaking called Operation Pastorius, the men sailed to America with orders to destroy factories producing war matériel. One spy, however, George Dasch, confessed to the FBI and betrayed his accomplices. A military tribunal condemned six of the men to death in the electric chair. For testifying against the others, Dasch earned thirty years in prison, whereas Ernest Burger, who had also given evidence at the trial, received a life sentence. "These men were fighting on the other side," said Dasch, a German-born American citizen, "and my turning them in was merely another way of fighting."

Richard Quirin   **Heinrich Heinck**   **Herbert Haupt**   **Hermann Neubauer**

pens and pencils, as well as rolls of electric cable along with fuses and timers. Two members of the U-boat crew paddled the saboteurs to shore.

At last the dinghy scraped on sand and the men scrambled up the beach with their gear. But just as they had begun to relax and breathe easily again, the beam of a flashlight cut through the murk. "What's going on out here?" a voice demanded. It belonged to twenty-one-year-old Seaman Second Class John Cullen of the United States Coast Guard, who was making a routine beach patrol.

The saboteurs had orders to kill anyone who got in their way and give the body to the sailors to carry back to the U-boat for disposal at sea. But the group's leader, George Dasch, decided against it. Thinking quickly, Dasch approached Cullen and explained, in as normal a voice as he could muster, that he and his companions were fishermen who had gotten lost in the fog. But then, unseen in the dark, the others began talking in German. Noticing Cullen's sudden alarm, Dasch grabbed the unarmed coastguardsman and stuck a pistol in his face. "You got a mother and a father, haven't you?" he hissed. "Wouldn't you like to see them again?" He pressed $265 in wadded bills into Cullen's hand: "Take this and have a good time. Forget what you've seen here." Terrified, Cullen backed away, then turned and fled, running for the Coast Guard station a half-mile away. Soon an armed patrol was heading for the beach.

By the time the patrol arrived, the Germans had changed into civilian clothes, buried their uniforms and explosives, and hustled inland. They found themselves on the edge of the town of Amagansett. Awakened by the roar of the retreating U-boat's diesel engines, some householders had turned on lights. But luckily nobody was abroad, and the saboteurs made it to the local railroad station. Shortly, an agent arrived and sold them tickets to Jamaica, the junction stop for all Long Island Railroad trains heading for New York City. About 6:30 a.m., the first westbound train of the day rattled in, and the saboteurs got aboard. Like the other commuters, each saboteur buried his face in the morning newspaper. At Pennsylvania Station, the team split up into pairs and headed for separate hotels, where they registered under their cover names.

Then, however, in a resounding anticlimax, Operation Pastorius suddenly collapsed, and none of its wildly ambitious acts of destruction ever took place. George Dasch, without a shred of warning, turned informer. On the evening after he arrived in New York City, he telephoned the FBI office in Foley Square, announcing that he had just arrived in the United States and had important information to relay. When pressed for details, he hung up, but not before promising, "I'll be in Washington within a week to deliver it personally to J. Edgar Hoover."

On June 19, Dasch took the train to Washington and called the FBI from his room at the Mayflower Hotel. He confessed everything, including the addresses of his cohorts in Manhattan and the fact that the other Pastorius team was loose in Florida. Within two weeks, the FBI had caught them all.

At the military tribunal appointed by President Roosevelt to try the saboteurs (the first such tribunal to be commissioned in the United States since the assassination of Abraham Lincoln in 1865), Dasch stoutly maintained that he loved America and had intended right from the start, even during his training in Germany, to blow the whistle. The tribunal sentenced him to thirty years in prison. Another of the Germans, who had

On the Russian front, a grim Wilhelm Canaris *(middle)* trudges to Adolf Hitler's office on June 30 to explain the collapse of Operation Pastorius in the United States three days earlier. With Canaris are two key aides, General Erwin Lahousen *(left)*, the Abwehr's head of sabotage, and Colonel Hans Piekenbrock, the Abwehr's chief of espionage.

After coming ashore near Jacksonville, Florida, on June 17, four of the Pastorius saboteurs buried their equipment in waterproof cases for retrieval later *(opposite, top)*. Among the explosives the FBI recovered from the beach were blocks of TNT, fuses, and bombs disguised as big chunks of coal *(bottom)*.

also provided evidence, received a life sentence. The other six were condemned to death. They all died in the electric chair and were buried in unmarked graves on government land in Washington, D.C.

Although Operation Pastorius was the Abwehr's most elaborate and sinister plot against the United States, it was far from the only one. In the year before America entered the war, and for some months afterward, the country was riddled with agents. In fact, Admiral Canaris's intelligence service was weaving webs of intrigue all over the globe. It was a gigantic effort that strained the Abwehr's capacities—as well as the police systems of the target nations.

Virtually all the agents in the United States were Germans who had emigrated to America, like the Pastorius saboteurs, or been born there of German parents. Some were opportunists out for money; others felt their first loyalty was to their fatherland. Most of the important agents had gone

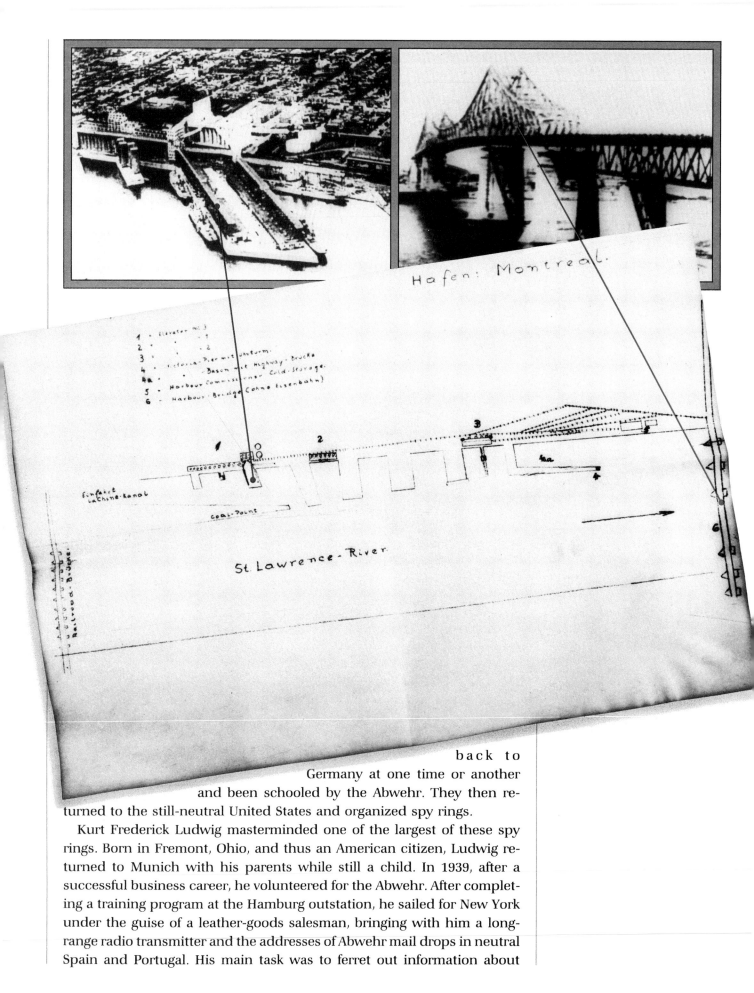

Hafen: Montreal.

1 = Elevator nr. 3
2 = " " 1
3 = " " 2
4 = Victoria-Pier mit Leuchtturm.
" = Bason mit Highway-Brücke
4a = " mit Cold-Storage.
5 = Harbour-Commissioner Cold-Storage.
6 = Harbour-Bridge (ohne Eisenbahn)

Einfahrt
Lachine-Kanal

Coal-Point

St. Lawrence-River.

Railroad-Bridge.

back to
Germany at one time or another
and been schooled by the Abwehr. They then re-
turned to the still-neutral United States and organized spy rings.

Kurt Frederick Ludwig masterminded one of the largest of these spy
rings. Born in Fremont, Ohio, and thus an American citizen, Ludwig returned to Munich with his parents while still a child. In 1939, after a
successful business career, he volunteered for the Abwehr. After complet-
ing a training program at the Hamburg outstation, he sailed for New York
under the guise of a leather-goods salesman, bringing with him a long-
range radio transmitter and the addresses of Abwehr mail drops in neutral
Spain and Portugal. His main task was to ferret out information about

During the 1930s, German spies prepared for possible war with the United States and Canada by sketching and photographing strategic sites in each country. At Montreal's harbor on the St. Lawrence River, German agents photographed grain elevators *(opposite, top left)* and a bridge *(opposite, top right)*, keying them to a schematic of the area *(opposite, bottom)*. In New York State, spies photographed the Westchester County waterworks *(above)*, a system that supplied New York City, and provided a sketch *(right)* with a cross section of an aqueduct. At Scarsdale, an agent photographed the train station *(above, right)*.

shipments of United States war matériel to Britain and to monitor American efforts to beef up its own armed forces.

Within weeks after arriving, Ludwig had recruited a team of informants, including Paul Borchardt, a retired German army major posing as a refugee from the Gestapo; René Froehlich, a recently drafted GI who was stationed on Governor's Island in New York Harbor; Lucy Boehmler, a member of the Nazi-backed German-American Youth Society; Carl Schroetter, a Swiss-born charter-boat skipper in Miami; and several members of the German-American Bund.

Ludwig himself drove around in a late-model automobile, often with Lucy Boehmler, gathering information on army camps, naval bases, and armaments factories. After a time, the two had assembled a file listing nearly every United States military installation, complete with the names of the principal officers, the numbers of personnel, the types of equipment, and the kinds of training.

For emergency use, Ludwig's car contained a portable shortwave radio, powerful enough to reach Abwehr listening posts in Brazil or U-boats prowling the Eastern Seaboard. Normally, however, he communicated with his handlers through typed letters addressed to the mail drops in Portugal and Spain. His messages in English, usually phony business correspondence, were interlined with real news handwritten in German in invisible ink. Occasionally Ludwig wrote in an obscure, nineteenth-century German shorthand, called Gabelsberger. He signed the letters Joe Kessler, or Joe K.

It was the letters that eventually brought him down. Airmail was carried by transatlantic clippers that flew from New York to Lisbon, stopping at Bermuda and the Azores en route. The British security coordination office on Bermuda routinely opened all envelopes passing through the island. For months, Ludwig's letters attracted no scrutiny. But eventually a few stilted, nonidiomatic English phrases caught the eye of the mail scanners. Still, the British could prove nothing. Ludwig's invisible ink, made out of a solution of Pyramidon, a brand of painkiller pills sold in drugstores, defied penetration. At last a chemist found a means to expose the hidden writing, and soon British intelligence had sent a sheaf of the incriminating intercepts to J. Edgar Hoover.

The FBI knew that Joe K. was one Kurt Ludwig and that he was probably in New York City—but exactly where? In a matter of weeks, though, Ludwig tripped himself up. Sensing that he was being shadowed, he decided to flee and contacted Schroetter in Miami about escaping to Cuba by boat. Schroetter vetoed the idea: FBI surveillance was too tight. Ludwig decided that his best chance was to drive his car to the West Coast, catch a ship bound for Japan, and get home to Germany from there. But the FBI got on his trail. G-men followed him to Ohio, where Ludwig had gone to pick up a copy of his American birth certificate—necessary in order to obtain a United States passport. Now the FBI knew for sure that their man was preparing to leave the country. Instead of arresting him, they decided to continue to tail him on the chance that he would reveal other spies. In Butte, Montana, Ludwig abandoned his car and took a Greyhound bus for the state of Washington. That was the end of the line. FBI agents arrested him in Seattle. In his pocket they found a black book containing the names of all the members of his ring, most of whom were soon in custody.

Another of the trained operatives sent to the United States by the Abwehr was Wilhelm Georg Debowski, a native of Germany who had served in the kaiser's forces during World War I. In 1922, Debowski, then a merchant seaman, jumped ship in Galveston, Texas, and went into hiding, assuming the name of William G. Sebold. He spent the next seventeen years working at a variety of jobs, including one at the Consolidated Aircraft Company in San Diego. In 1939, he returned to Germany to see his family—and was recruited by the Abwehr. To his recruiters, Sebold seemed a special prize because of his familiarity with American aircraft production.

Sebold was given the Abwehr's standard seven-week training course: coding and decoding, using invisible inks, operating a shortwave trans-

In March 1942, nineteen-year-old Lucy Boehmler leaves a Manhattan courtroom with a federal marshal after being sentenced to five years in prison for espionage. Kurt Ludwig *(above)*, leader of a German spy ring, drew the naive young woman into his enterprise with tales of the adventurous life she would lead.

mitter, and taking microphotographs of documents that reduced a page to the size of a pencil dot. He was then put aboard an ocean liner for New York, where he arrived on February 6, 1940. In his pockets were a false passport in the name of his alias, William G. Sawyer, and the addresses of four German agents already busy around the city. His orders, delivered before he left Germany by his Abwehr case officer, Captain Hermann Sandel, were to establish an office in Manhattan as a collecting point for information and to start sending it across the Atlantic by radio.

All this Sebold did, renting an office in the Knickerbocker Building at 42d Street and Broadway and setting up a radio transmitter in Centerport, Long Island. He contacted the veteran spies of the New York area, Frederick Duquesne, Carl Reuper, Hermann Lang, and Everett Roeder. The latter two had managed to steal partial blueprints for the Norden bombsight in the late 1930s. A young woman named Lilly Stein served Sebold as courier and recruiter of new informants.

In early April, Sebold alerted the Hamburg outstation that he was ready to start sending information. Through the late spring and summer of 1940, messages flowed from Centerport. "The Belgian ship *Ville d'Ablon* departed with copper, machine parts, motors," read one coded transmission, adding that the "English steamer *Britannic* departs Tuesday with aeroengines and twelve heavy bombers." In short order, Sebold, known in Hamburg by the code name Tramp, had become one of the Abwehr's most important spies.

Apparently. But Sebold had outfoxed the foxes. Even before leaving Germa-

This radio used by German spies consisted of three stainless-steel compartments that together were no bigger than a small briefcase. On the left is the receiver, in the center, the battery, and on the right, a transmitter that enabled agents anywhere in Europe to send messages to Abwehr headquarters.

ny, he had secretly gone to the American consulate in Cologne and explained what was afoot. Once in New York, he contacted the FBI, conniving with its agents to install a two-way mirror in his office so that a hidden movie camera could film every visit. FBI agents also took over the Centerport radio, broadcasting false or innocuous reports. In June 1941, the FBI hauled in the net, capturing no fewer than thirty-three agents.

News of Sebold's treachery quickly reached Abwehr headquarters. Major Nikolaus Ritter, head of air intelligence at the Hamburg outstation, shouted in fury, "The bastard! The traitor!" "But Ritter," replied Hans Piekenbrock, the chief of the secret intelligence section, "by your own principles, Tramp was no traitor. He was a man who worked for his new fatherland."

The demise of the Ludwig and Sebold networks crippled Abwehr operations in the United States and damaged German-American relations. Banner headlines reading "Spy rings smashed" appeared in newspapers across the nation, causing a wave of anti-German feeling. It also shocked many Abwehr officers who had assumed that the American security forces were too inefficient to catch anybody. And it weakened the Abwehr at home by providing new justification for attacks by Reinhard Heydrich and his SD.

Still, some lone wolves continued to operate in the United States. Among them was a white-haired little man in his late fifties named Simon Emil Koedel, who had achieved the rank of major in the Abwehr. He had been filing reports from the United States since 1936 and had proved himself a clever jack-of-all-trades. He watched shipping in New York Harbor, often brazenly peering through binoculars while riding the Staten Island Ferry. He gained membership in the American Ordnance Association, a trade group of armaments makers, which gave entrée to many munitions plants and put him on the mailing list for War Department publications. He curried friendships with members of Congress who had inside knowledge of military affairs. In all, Koedel sent the Abwehr more than 600 fact-filled messages. One of them—an analysis of how Allied convoys were organized—was perhaps the most valuable single report ever dispatched by any German spy in the United States. Koedel and his foster daughter, Marie, pieced the document together from bits of information they had gleaned from bibulous sailors in waterfront bars. Koedel and Marie were finally arrested by the FBI in October of 1944. He was sentenced to fifteen years in prison; Marie received seven and a half years.

Even at that late date in the war, German intelligence was still trying to infiltrate America. On November 28, 1944, a long-range submarine, U-1230, surfaced off the coast of Maine and began inching past the islands in Frenchman Bay near the fashionable resort of Bar Harbor. Inside the narrow bay, the U-boat submerged again, waiting for nightfall, then glided toward an inlet where its two passengers could get ashore in a rubber boat.

One of the passengers was William C. Colepaugh, a twenty-six-year-old American from Niantic, Connecticut. Dazzled by Hitler's promise of a new world order, Colepaugh had made his way to Lisbon as a merchant sailor, jumped ship, sought out the local Abwehr office, and was soon on his way to Germany. The other passenger was a German named Erich Gimpel. Both

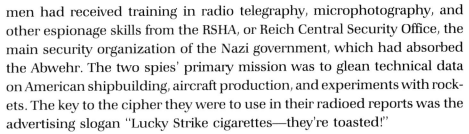

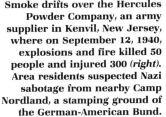

Smoke drifts over the Hercules Powder Company, an army supplier in Kenvil, New Jersey, where on September 12, 1940, explosions and fire killed 50 people and injured 300 *(right)*. Area residents suspected Nazi sabotage from nearby Camp Nordland, a stamping ground of the German-American Bund.

men had received training in radio telegraphy, microphotography, and other espionage skills from the RSHA, or Reich Central Security Office, the main security organization of the Nazi government, which had absorbed the Abwehr. The two spies' primary mission was to glean technical data on American shipbuilding, aircraft production, and experiments with rockets. The key to the cipher they were to use in their radioed reports was the advertising slogan "Lucky Strike cigarettes—they're toasted!"

Getting ashore in the submarine's rubber dinghy, Colepaugh and Gimpel walked up a beach, plunged into a woods dusted with early snow, and found a dirt road leading to U.S. Route 1, the highway running from Maine to Florida. There they encountered a taxi driver who took them to Bangor. From Bangor they went by train to Portland and on to Boston and New York, where they sublet an apartment on Manhattan's Beekman Place.

For the first time, they could relax. And relax Colepaugh did—with a vengeance. Drawing on the $60,000 that he had assured his SD handlers was necessary in order to survive for a year in New York City, he went on a spending spree, buying an expensive suit, eating at posh restaurants, drinking in nightclubs, and picking up girls. His espionage mission did not seem very important amid the glitter of New York at Christmastime. But it

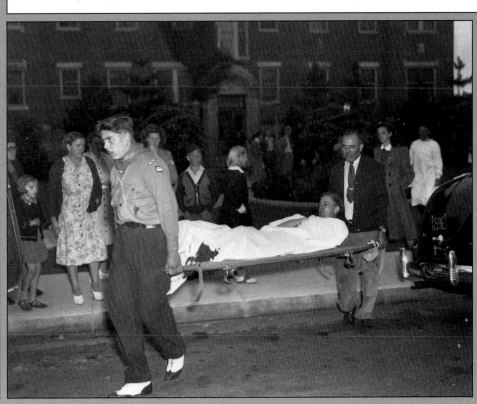

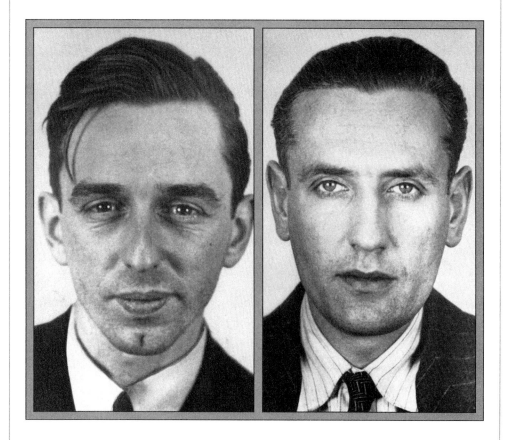

FBI agents in New York City had spies Erich Gimpel *(near left)* and William Colepaugh in custody one month after they emerged from a U-boat near Bar Harbor, Maine, in November 1944. Colepaugh turned himself in and then fingered his partner.

did seem increasingly dangerous. Colepaugh knew that he faced death if he was caught. Also, the newspapers were full of stories about the Battle of the Bulge, Hitler's surprise counterattack against United States army forces in Belgium's Forest of Ardennes. Reading them, Colepaugh was afflicted with pangs of patriotism. He did not like the idea that American troops were being battered by the Germans. On December 23, he ditched Gimpel in the Christmas crowd at Rockefeller Center and made his way to Queens. He located an old high-school friend, confessed his secret mission, and asked his friend to telephone the FBI. Soon an agent arrived to interview this strange turncoat—who eagerly offered all the information the FBI needed to find and arrest his colleague Gimpel. Both men were tried by a military court and sentenced to death, but President Harry Truman commuted the sentences.

The scenes of German agents coming ashore on American beaches had been played out before—on the coasts of England and Scotland. Beginning in 1940, the Abwehr used every means possible to infiltrate agents into the British Isles. Many arrived courtesy of the Luftwaffe, parachuting down on meadows and moorlands. Others, posing as businessmen or refugees, reached Britain on commercial airplanes or merchant ships that traveled between Lisbon and England's south coast. A few of the infiltrators were saboteurs, but the majority were spies in pursuit of information about

Britain's armed forces—the RAF's planes and their performance, and the organization, equipment, strength, and location of army units. The spies were to send the most vital intelligence back to Germany immediately by tapping out messages in Morse code on the radio sets many carried with them. Less urgent information would go to Lisbon or Madrid in letters written in invisible ink.

The Abwehr was rebuilding its intelligence network in Britain from the ground up. In 1935, Hitler, viewing England as a possible ally, forbade intensive spying in Great Britain and did not reverse the prohibition until 1937. Shortly before the war, the Abwehr, according to its own records, had employed at one time or another no fewer than 253 operatives of all kinds

On a beach in Maine, the young Harvard Hodgkins studies the spot where the spies Gimpel and Colepaugh came ashore. Driving home from a dance, the high-school student spotted the two strangers and followed their tracks to the sea. He then alerted his father, Deputy Sheriff Dana Hodgkins, who notified the FBI.

Lethal Tools of the Trade

Because the Abwehr often trained its agents hastily, weapons and explosives supplied by the organization's technicians were designed to be simple and easy to use. And since the devices had to be concealed, they were also compact; a spy's personal arsenal might include a knife that could be hidden in the palm of a hand, and a blackjack, or "cosh"—for knocking an enemy unconscious—that could be concealed up a coat sleeve. The simplicity of these miniature weapons made them highly reliable—a trait much appreciated by the operatives. With only one chance to save his life or blow up a bridge, an agent needed equipment that worked the first time.

"Coshes" were telescoping steel springs. When compressed, the device could be hidden inside a jacket sleeve; the user simply gripped the weapon and whipped his arm forward to extend the cosh to its full length, as much as sixteen inches. Some agents carried the compact model (*near right*) or the rubber truncheon (*center*) to stun their victims, but others wielded a lead-tipped version (*far right*) lethal enough to crack a skull.

This finger-size knife (*above*) was carried in a sheath sewn inside a pocket or under a coat lapel.

To open a gravity knife (*below*), the holder simply pressed a catch on top of its wooden grip and flicked his wrist. The spike was useful for untangling knots in parachute lines.

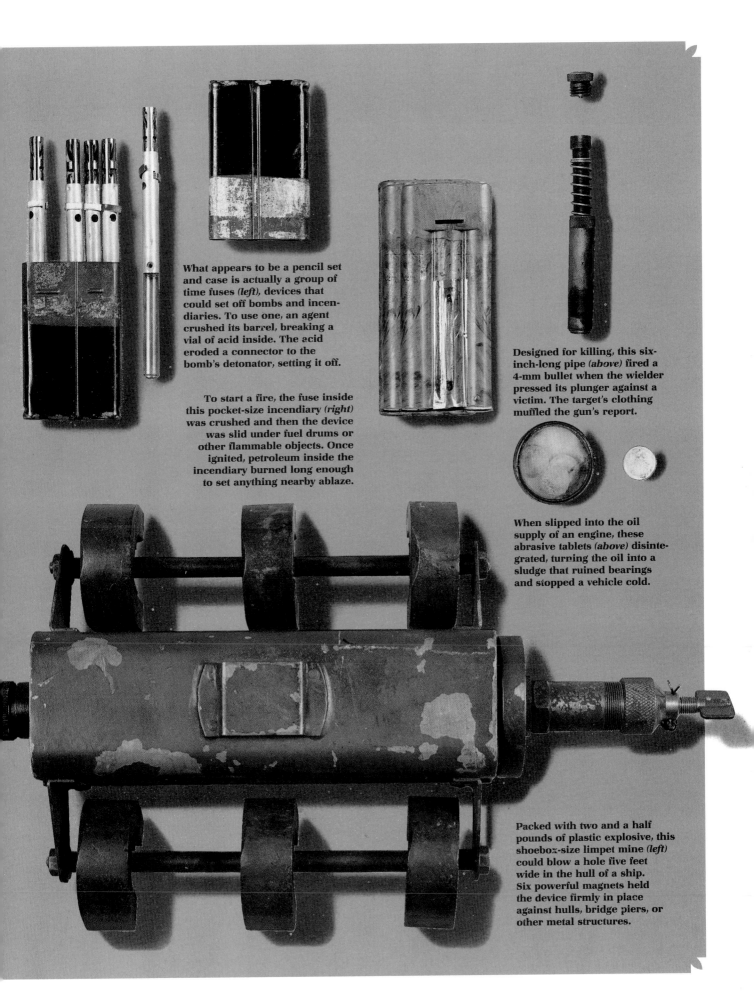

What appears to be a pencil set and case is actually a group of time fuses (*left*), devices that could set off bombs and incendiaries. To use one, an agent crushed its barrel, breaking a vial of acid inside. The acid eroded a connector to the bomb's detonator, setting it off.

To start a fire, the fuse inside this pocket-size incendiary (*right*) was crushed and then the device was slid under fuel drums or other flammable objects. Once ignited, petroleum inside the incendiary burned long enough to set anything nearby ablaze.

Designed for killing, this six-inch-long pipe (*above*) fired a 4-mm bullet when the wielder pressed its plunger against a victim. The target's clothing muffled the gun's report.

When slipped into the oil supply of an engine, these abrasive tablets (*above*) disintegrated, turning the oil into a sludge that ruined bearings and stopped a vehicle cold.

Packed with two and a half pounds of plastic explosive, this shoebox-size limpet mine (*left*) could blow a hole five feet wide in the hull of a ship. Six powerful magnets held the device firmly in place against hulls, bridge piers, or other metal structures.

in Britain. Sometimes posing as sightseers, they had helped German military planners locate most of the primary airfields, port facilities, munitions factories, and oil-storage facilities in eastern England. From the fragments of information submitted by them, the Abwehr and other German intelligence analysts had pieced together a fairly accurate picture of British war capabilities. But when the war began in September 1939, the British police and other security agencies swiftly rounded up virtually every alien in the country. About 600 of them were classed as "unreliables" and deported or detained. Another 6,800 "uncertains" were subject to continued scrutiny. The crackdown dismantled the Abwehr's network of informants in Britain and ended the flow of reliable information.

For a time it did not seem to matter. Hitler was convinced that the British would come to their senses and make peace, especially after the Wehrmacht's lightning occupation of Norway in April of 1940, followed in May and June by the swift conquest of Belgium, the Netherlands, and France. But the British remained stubbornly defiant. General Alfred Jodl, OKW chief of operations, demanded that Canaris send in fresh teams of spies to supply target information for the Luftwaffe's bombers and tactical intelligence for Operation Sea Lion, the planned cross-channel invasion that was to take place as soon as the Luftwaffe could gain air superiority.

It was an impractical demand. Not only were Germany and England at war, making the insertion of spies risky in the extreme, but there was no time to find reliable new men for the job. Canaris nevertheless ordered Ritter and Herbert Wichmann of the Hamburg outstation to recruit, train, and equip a whole fresh crew. "But that's impossible, Herr Admiral," Wichmann objected, to which Canaris replied, "This is one time when the impossible must be possible." The Abwehr dubbed the proposed invasion of spies Operation Lena, but skeptics within the agency privately referred to it as Operation *Himmelfahrt*, or Operation Trip to Heaven.

Wichmann and Ritter set out to follow orders. Their first move was to send Lieut. Colonel Karl Praetorius, chief of the outstation's economics section and its best recruiter, scouring the newly conquered countries for potential agents who could pass as refugees from the Nazis. The candidates Praetorius chose were given quick courses in cryptography and in the operation of the compact radio sets, called Afus, that the Telefunken Electronics Corporation had made especially for the Abwehr. The fledgling spies were then sent on their way, even though many lacked the detailed knowledge of the target country that is essential to a spy's safety and success. The results were predictable.

The first agents to go, four men divided into two teams, were ferried at night from Boulogne to the Kentish coast in a trawler. With amateurish zeal,

Major Herbert Wichmann, head of the Abwehr's Hamburg outstation, was responsible for recruiting, training, and equipping German spies and saboteurs bound for England in the summer and fall of 1940.

the leader of one of the teams, a Franco-German named José Rudolf Waldberg, got out his Afu set and sent a cheerful arrival message back to Germany, which could easily have been intercepted by the British. It was not the radio transmission, however, that undid Waldberg's team. Rather it was a mistake made by his comrade, Carl Meier, who entered a British pub at nine o'clock the next morning and asked for a glass of cider. The proprietress realized at once that Meier was a foreigner; no Englishman would have expected a pub to be open that early. She told Meier to come back at ten—and phoned the police, who collared Meier and Waldberg as well. The other team also suffered an ignominious fate. They blundered into a bivouac of the Somerset Light Infantry and were promptly arrested.

Several of the other hastily trained teams proved equally inept. One pair, flown to the Scottish coast in a seaplane, got wet wading ashore. When they purchased rail tickets at a nearby depot, the agent noticed their soaked clothes. Suspicious, he telephoned the local constable, who found telltale mistakes in the pair's forged British identity cards. The constable took the spies to the local police headquarters, where a quick search produced a

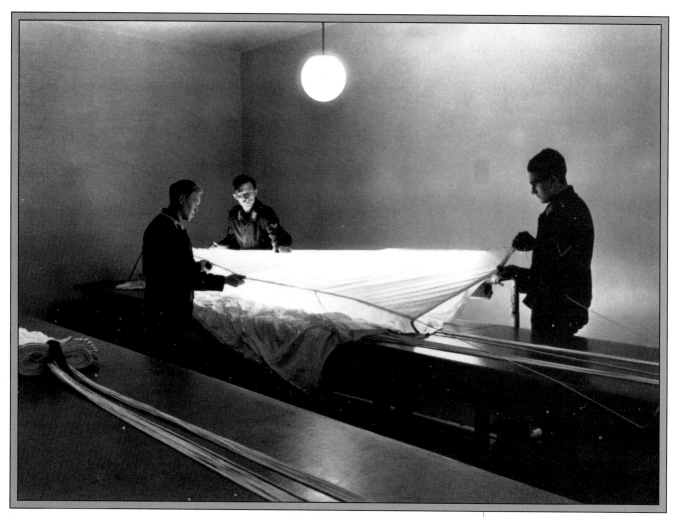

half-eaten German sausage, a Mauser pistol, and an Afu radio set neatly hidden in a suitcase.

After a time, however, the Abwehr recruits seemed to be having better luck. One was a twenty-six-year-old Dane named Wolf Schmidt, who went by the alias Hans Hansen. A fervent Nazi, Hansen welcomed the chance to spy on Britain. His partner was a tall Finn named Goesta Caroli. Arriving in Hamburg, the two men reported to Ritter. "I think you know what you have volunteered for," Ritter warned. "You know you are putting your lives in the balance." They knew, Hansen replied, and were still eager to go.

Ritter lodged his charges in a small Hamburg hotel, called the Klopstock, that served as an Abwehr boardinghouse, and had instructors drill them in Morse code, aircraft and gun-caliber recognition, and English geography. By early August 1940, the pair were at a Luftwaffe airfield in France where they met Captain Karl Gartenfeld, a pilot who specialized in secret night missions. Soon Gartenfeld flew Caroli across the Channel in his black-painted Heinkel 111 bomber and dropped him over England.

Several days later, Caroli belatedly called in. There had been a mishap; he had injured his leg on landing and needed help. On September 19, Hansen parachuted safely, alighting outside a village in Cambridgeshire. Ritter decided to contact a trusted Abwehr spy in London, code-named Johnny, who had somehow eluded the Scotland Yard crackdown. Soon Ritter received a report that Johnny had dispatched a subagent to locate Hansen and Caroli and provide Caroli with medical attention. Johnny had

also arranged to rent an apartment in Cambridge where Caroli and Hansen could safely lie up.

After broadcasting a few messages, Caroli went underground. But Hansen continued to send regular reports—more than 1,000 over the next several years. In time, he proved to be almost as annoying as he was productive. He constantly nagged Ritter for more money, and sometimes he declared himself to be off-duty. "Won't be reporting for a couple of days," he once radioed. "I'm getting drunk tonight."

Two other new agents also seemed to be faring well. These were a pair of Norwegians, Olaf Klausen and Jack Berg, both members of Vidkun Quisling's Fascist party. Flown to the Scottish coast in a seaplane, the Norwegians paddled ashore and were soon reporting from the London area. Another agent, who was assigned the task of blowing up the de Havilland aircraft factory at Hatfield, successfully parachuted into a Cam-

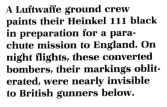

A Luftwaffe ground crew paints their Heinkel 111 black in preparation for a parachute mission to England. On night flights, these converted bombers, their markings obliterated, were nearly invisible to British gunners below.

bridgeshire meadow. And still more entered England: twenty-five agents during the latter months of 1940, and seventeen in 1941.

Officials at the Hamburg outstation congratulated themselves on achieving the impossible. They never suspected the truth—that they had been double-crossed. MI-5, the British counterespionage service, knew all about the German agents as soon as they landed—and even before. What seemed an Abwehr triumph turned out to be a fiasco.

The pivotal figure in the hoax was none other than Johnny, the apparently reliable Abwehr agent in London. In reality, Johnny was a forty-year-old, skirt-chasing, Scotch-drinking Welshman named Arthur George Owens. Like many Welshmen, Owens professed to dislike the English, and in the late 1930s, he made several trips across the Channel to offer his services to the Abwehr. At the same time, however, Owens was working for the British admiralty. When he became discontent with his admiralty pay, he thought nothing of selling information to the Abwehr. At any rate, on the day Britain declared war, Owens contacted the Special Branch at Scotland Yard and said he was ready to help Britain again, revealing the location of his hidden radio. Scotland Yard, uncertain which side the slippery Owens was on, lodged him for safekeeping in Wandsworth Prison. MI-5 agents interviewed him and insisted that he prove his good intentions by contacting Hamburg on his radio. This Owens did, operating the Afu in his cell and starting his message with his favorite German phrase, "Ein Glas Bier." From then on, Owens was a double agent working for British intelligence.

It was largely through Owens's radio traffic with Hamburg that MI-5 learned the identities of the German spies who were already in England and the arrival dates and locations of the incoming agents. Before long, the security forces were arresting the spies almost as soon as they set foot on British soil.

MI-5 turned a number of these new arrivals into double agents. Hansen was among the first. He and Caroli were arrested shortly after Ritter asked Owens to send help to the injured Caroli. Hansen not only agreed to work with MI-5 but became a star operative. As Tate, his British code name, he was soon hard at work sending messages to Ritter and receiving instructions in return, every word monitored by his handler.

Klausen and Berg also became double agents, as did eventually more

Arthur Owens, a self-described "Welsh nationalist bitterly opposed to everything English," was Germany's most trusted spy in Britain. After his arrest, however, he became a double agent, unmasking other German spies and revealing Abwehr plans to the British.

In this house near Cambridge, England, British authorities held the spy Goesta Caroli prisoner in January 1941. After two suicide attempts, the desperate agent managed to overpower his guard and flee—only to be recaptured about twenty miles away.

than three dozen other German spies. All were given code names by their British controllers. Klausen and Berg became Mutt and Jeff; others were dubbed Rainbow and the Snark, Mullet and Giraffe, Careless and Balloon.

The British pulled off this remarkable double cross by subjecting each captured spy to an interrogation. Those judged unfit to be double agents were simply imprisoned; the others were offered a stark option: They could either become double agents or be executed as spies. Most opted to save their skins—although, in fact, the British used the death penalty sparingly, preferring to jail those who refused. An MI-5 case officer monitored the newly recruited double agent's every action and helped him write out, encode, and send the proper messages to Hamburg. "Only unremitting care and some psychological finesse could coax a converted parachutist into a better way of thinking," noted a British spymaster.

The best of all the double agents was a Spaniard named Juan Pujol García, dubbed Garbo for his superb ability to act the faithful German spy. A veteran of both the Nationalist and the Republican armies in the Spanish Civil War, García had developed an intense hatred for Hitler. He contacted Abwehr officers in Lisbon, convincing them he would be a valuable spy in Britain. The Abwehr duly sent him, and he immediately began working for MI-5. Garbo and his case officer, a Spanish-speaking Briton named Tomás Harris, invented an entire ring of fictitious agents, all supposedly recruited by Garbo and reporting to him from every part of the British Isles. Over a period of more than three years, Garbo and Harris sent some 2,400

messages, and the Abwehr swallowed every mendacious report.

At the top of this whole system, called the Double Cross or the XX, was a committee made up of intelligence experts and representatives from the various British armed services who decided what sorts of information the double agents and their case officers should reveal. The information had to be plausible, even factual, but could not reveal too much. Ideally, the items would elicit useful information about Abwehr plans as well as deceive the Germans about Allied strengths and intentions. The XX committee and the case officers managed this juggling act so deftly that Ritter and other Abwehr officers were completely fooled.

The activities of the XX scheme reached a crescendo in the months leading up to D-Day. For this climactic effort, MI-5 marshaled its best and most believable double agents including Mutt, Tate, Garbo, and another superb faker, Dusko Popov, known as Tricycle. Huge amounts of misleading information flowed across the Channel. Most notably, the agents conjured two entire Allied army corps out of thin air and persuaded the German high command that one of them was poised to make the main landing at the Pas de Calais (Strait of Dover), the English Channel's narrowest point. The German generals were so convinced Calais was the main target that they kept several divisions there for weeks after the real Allied armies had stormed ashore at Normandy.

Admiral Canaris, an expert on Latin America, decided to make Brazil the center of his intelligence operations in the Southern Hemisphere. Many large German firms had offices in Brazil, and almost 900,000 people of German birth or ancestry lived there. In addition, the South Atlantic convoy routes ran alongside the Brazilian coast, and radio transmitters within the country could beam signals by the shortest transoceanic route to Europe.

The Abwehr stepped up its efforts in Brazil as soon as the war began, originating a number of spy rings in Rio de Janeiro and other cities. The first important cell was headed by Albrecht Gustav Engels, a dapper German-born engineer who had emigrated to Brazil after World War I and managed the local offices of AEG, a German electrical company. Signed up by the Abwehr during a vacation trip to Europe in the late 1930s, Engels returned to Brazil and got busy, under the code name Alfredo. He had a powerful radio transmitter built and gathered a stable of informants.

One of his spies was Herbert von Heyer, also a German-born Brazilian, who worked in the shipping department of a German firm and had contacts on Rio's waterfront who could furnish information about naval traffic. Heyer, in turn, found Hans Sievert, who lived in the northern Brazilian port city of Recife and had connections in Natal, another port in the north.

British soldiers take two German agents into custody in the south of England. Many spies were caught just hours after reaching the country. "You must expect losses in this kind of business," wrote an Abwehr official. "But even if only one of them gets through and sends back valuable information, the investment has been worthwhile."

Sievert's contribution was vital: Recife was a regular stop for convoys headed for North Africa and for British and American warships, and Natal had several airfields that were used after June of 1941 as refueling points for American warplanes being flown across the Atlantic to West Africa and thence to England, Egypt, or Russia. Engels and his radio operators were soon sending reports to Hamburg—and they became even busier after the FBI crackdown silenced the Abwehr apparatus in the United States.

Friedrich Kempter, a German who had lived in Brazil for more than a decade, headed a second network. Contacted by the Abwehr through a German-Brazilian company, he adopted the code name König, or King. Kempter and his Austrian business partner, Heriberto Müller, had set up a commercial information firm, appropriately called Rapid Information

Ltd., which became a front for Kempter's activities. By August of 1940, Müller became a willing partner in the spy business as well.

The pair assembled a team of German-born Brazilians to spy on shipping and other activities in Rio, then found an ally, Karl Fink, to report from Recife and Natal. Building a radio with the help of a Telefunken technician, Kempter began to flood Hamburg with reports. One message relayed from Buenos Aires reported two large cargo vessels departing the River Plate. Both ships were subsequently sunk by U-boats operating in the South Atlantic, possibly as a result of the report.

The Abwehr was pleased, awarding Kempter a medal *in absentia.* Nonetheless, the Hamburg outstation decided to set up additional spy rings in Brazil. One of them was headed by a Latvian-born German named Franz Walther Jordan. Jordan took a steamer from Bordeaux to Rio, where he was welcomed by two members of the city's German community, Hans Holl and Herbert Winterstein. With their help, Jordan found lodging at a boarding-house in the colorful beach district of Ipanema and began sending radio reports to Hamburg.

Still not satisfied, the Abwehr set up four more rings, headed by four new recruits: Theodor Schlegel, a German, Josef Starziczny, a Pole, Othmar Gamillscheg, an Austrian-Brazilian, and Janos Salomon, a Hungarian. Starziczny proved especially energetic—and disruptive. Trained in Hamburg by Wichmann and Ritter, he had hardly stepped off the ship that smuggled him into Brazil before signing up Albert Schwab, a shipping expert, to watch the Rio docks, and another confederate, Karl Mugge, to run the group's radio and to report from Recife. Starziczny then opened up contact with the German consul in Santos to provide information from that city. By June 1941, the new spy was sending out 100 messages per month.

Starziczny's dynamic approach annoyed the methodical Albrecht Engels, who was already upset about having so many new spies in his territory. Engels appealed to Hamburg to make Starziczny join his own Rio operation, then tried to intimidate him into cooperating. The abrasive new spy refused, causing a breach in the German ranks. To make matters worse,

Starziczny's extravagant lifestyle outraged members of his own cell—and made him increasingly unpopular with penurious Abwehr accountants back in Berlin. He drove a flashy 1940 Oldsmobile and lived in a large house in the posh Copacabana district with his Brazilian mistress, whom he refused to give up, despite warnings that having any stranger privy to Abwehr secrets was asking for trouble.

The frictions created by Starziczny helped bring down the Abwehr's intelligence structure in Brazil. The trouble began when his rival, Engels, contrived to deny him access to a shortwave radio. Angry, Starziczny tried to get another set in operation, going himself to a radio store to purchase a component. The store's proprietor, suspicious of this stranger who spoke no Portuguese and wanted the sort of wavemeter used in powerful transmitters, notified the police, who began looking into Starziczny's activities and associations.

By then, however, the sheer volume of the radio traffic generated by the German agents had caught the attention of the Allies. By late 1941, the British and American intelligence services had intercepted hundreds of messages, and the Allied governments put pressure on Brazil's president, Getulio Vargas, to put an end to the German spying. But Vargas did little until after Pearl Harbor. Then, with his powerful neighbor to the north at war with the Axis, he severed diplomatic relations with Berlin, Rome, and Tokyo and, despite resistance from pro-Nazi members of his cabinet, ordered a crackdown.

The first arrest came on December 18, when the police picked up Erwin Backhaus, Schlegel's observer in Recife. Schlegel's ring broke up, and Salomon's operation collapsed soon afterward. Other rings tried to carry on, hiding their radio transmitters in the countryside and otherwise covering their tracks. "We are destroying all compromising documents, maintaining radio operations as long as possible. Heil Hitler!" the dedicated Friedrich Kempter signaled Hamburg. By February, even Kempter was alarmed. His man in Recife, Karl Fink, had been arrested. The Abwehr warned Kempter to reduce his radio traffic and report only vital news.

The arrests multiplied in mid-February, when the Rio police collared two subagents working for Herbert von Heyer. The men implicated Heyer and Rapid Information Ltd. In early March, Josef Starziczny's unwise visit to the radio shop proved his undoing. Following leads provided by the shop's proprietor, the police arrested seven subagents and, some days later, nabbed Starziczny himself in his handsome house along with his radio, code books, and microdot instructions.

Despite the increasing heat, the dedicated Kempter kept trying to tap out messages to Hamburg. So did the Engels group, even though its sources of information in Recife and Natal had dried up. Disaster finally struck in mid-March with a wave of arrests. Several of Engels's associates were rounded up, then Engels himself. The same day, Kempter was arrested and his transmitter seized. Still more arrests followed. The German embassy in Rio could only inform Abwehr headquarters of the catastrophe—and send an obliquely worded alarm warning agents outside Brazil to stop sending messages to their cohorts in that country. Engels's workshop had exploded, the message read, rendering the "largest part of his staff unfit for work." Engels himself had become a "victim of his trade."

Evidence against the spies piled up. Starziczny had unwisely kept records of all his activities and contacts, and the police, using torture, wrenched information about the last few uncaught spies from the prisoners. The ringleaders were given stiff jail sentences of twenty years or more. Although none served the full term, all stayed behind bars for the remainder of the war.

A similar fate befell German efforts in Mexico. In the late 1930s, the Abwehr had organized two large networks in Mexico City, whose radio operators regularly passed along intelligence on American and British naval and military matters and relayed messages from German agents in the United States. In 1939, one of the Mexican operatives, Dr. Joachim Hertslet, negotiated a trade pact to purchase Mexican oil for Germany, despite an embargo on selling to that country by Shell and Standard Oil. After the war began, the tankers carrying the oil to Germany took devious routes past the British naval blockade. Another agent, Karl Rekowski, recruited Mexicans to sabotage American factories.

But as early as the summer of 1940, the Mexican operation began fraying at the edges. The main problem was financial. Wartime restrictions made it difficult to transfer money from one country to another, and a British-imposed currency freeze, abetted by the United States, made it even harder. Canaris finally prevailed upon Mussolini to give the Abwehr access to some $4 million in Italian funds in American banks. Italian couriers managed to withdraw the funds, packing the bills in diplomatic pouches. But much of the cash earmarked for Mexico City was confiscated at the Texas-Mexico border by the Mexican secret police. The money vanished until after the war, when it mysteriously turned up in a Mexican government account. Meanwhile, the Abwehr in Mexico simply went broke.

With the demise of operations in Mexico and Brazil, Argentina became the center of espionage in South America. The main organizer there was Johann Siegfried Becker, who was not an Abwehr agent but a member of Reinhard Heydrich's rival organization, the SD. Becker came to Argentina in June of 1940 as the SD chief for Latin America. With his deputy, Heinz

In 1942, Johann Becker *(inset)*, an SD agent in Argentina, set up a radio station on this farm near Buenos Aires. He kept his transmitter in a straw-covered pit inside the farm's chicken coop *(right)*. According to a colleague, Becker was the "only real professional agent" working in the Argentinian network.

Lang, he set up shop in the center of the Buenos Aires business district.

Despite opposition from German Foreign Ministry officials, who viewed the SD's South American foray as an impingement on their turf, Becker and Lang put together an effective organization that survived not only the destruction of the Abwehr rings but also the ouster, in 1943, of the diplomats themselves. That year, Becker had fifty-three radio operators, informants, and other helpers working for him, plus more agents reporting from Chile, Paraguay, and Bolivia.

The various schemes cooked up by the Abwehr in the Middle East were all related in one way or another to Hitler's dream of cutting off Great Britain's access to the resources of the region and its route to India. One ambitious plan aimed at overthrowing the British government in Egypt and replacing it with a pro-German Egyptian regime. The chief orchestrator was a twenty-seven-year-old lawyer named Karl-Heinz Kraemer, who came to Cairo in November of 1940 after the Italian army's advance had stalled at the Libyan-Egyptian border. Nikolaus Ritter, in Hamburg, sent along a Hungarian Egyptologist, Count Ladislaus de Almaszy, to assist him. Through Almaszy, Kraemer contacted a group of Egyptian army officers eager to free their country from British control. Chief among them was the commander of the Egyptian army, General Masri Pasha; also involved were two ambitious junior officers, Gamal Abdel Nasser and Anwar Sadat, both future presidents of Egypt.

Kraemer's first exploit was to obtain from Masri Pasha the British plans for the defense of the Western Desert. This backfired, however, when a British unit overran an Axis headquarters and captured a copy of the purloined plans. Knowing the source of the security leak, the British fired Masri Pasha and placed him under arrest.

This action only strengthened the general's resolve. The Abwehr plotted to help Masri Pasha escape so that he might lead an Egyptian army of liberation into Cairo, side by side with General Erwin Rommel's Afrikakorps. Again, Kraemer was the chief conspirator, devising ways to abduct Masri Pasha and get him to Rommel's headquarters. Kraemer almost succeeded. On one occasion, a Luftwaffe plane disguised with Royal Air Force markings flew to an abandoned airfield in the desert outside Cairo. But Masri Pasha's automobile broke down on the way to the rendezvous. On the next try, Kraemer arranged for an Egyptian air force plane, flown by a pilot who was known to be reliably anti-British, to whisk Masri Pasha into Libya. By this time, though, Britain's chief of security in Egypt, Captain A. W. Sansom, had penetrated the plot. British troops showed up at the airfield just as the plane was taking off. Instead of leading an army of liberation, Masri Pasha and his fellow conspirators spent the rest of the war languishing in a British jail.

In another ambitious scheme, concocted in September 1941 after the Afrikakorps's advance toward Egypt had been stalled, the Abwehr sneaked a spy into Palestine to report on the strength of the British reinforcements being gathered there. For this important job, Canaris chose the most unlikely agent employed by the Germans during the entire conflict.

He was Paul Ernst Fackenheim, a highly decorated World War I army officer who afterward had become a successful hardware salesman. But Fackenheim was a Jew—and to recruit him as a spy, Canaris's men first had to get him released from Dachau concentration camp. Somehow the Abwehr managed this extraordinary maneuver despite violent objections from the SS. After being released from the brutal work details at Dachau and spending time in the camp hospital, Fackenheim found himself being interviewed by a courtly young Abwehr officer. Within hours of their talk, the flabbergasted ex-prisoner was outside the barbed wire fences and speeding toward Munich in a large Mercedes. There he was put aboard a train bound for Brussels. After a brief stay under Abwehr protection, he was given pocket money and new clothes and flown to Berlin. Perhaps most amazing of all, his Abwehr instructors called him Herr, a courtesy not accorded Jews in Hitler's Germany.

In fact, the Abwehr had chosen Fackenheim precisely because he was Jewish—and would therefore be welcomed by Zionist settlers when he arrived in Palestine. The Abwehr's detailed file noted that he was fluent in several foreign languages, including English and Hebrew, and that his hobby was gourmet cooking. His code name would be Koch—"cook" in German.

After training in Berlin, Fackenheim flew to German-occupied Athens where Hans Müller, an Abwehr officer he had met in Berlin, gave him further coaching in operating an Afu radio set, using invisible inks, and identifying the different types of British aircraft and tanks. Finally, he was taught the basics of parachute jumping.

Fackenheim's stay in Athens had its alarming moments. He was accosted in a restaurant by German civilians who tried to get him drunk and engage him in pointed conversation. Fackenheim realized they were Gestapo agents out to trap him when one morning he awoke to find a venomous-

Using microphotography, spies for the Abwehr could squeeze a page of written material onto a swatch of film the size of a printed period. This microdot could then be hidden within a letter or on an envelope (*above, encircled*) and mailed undetected.

looking man in his hotel room. The intruder insulted him, calling him a "filthy Jewish bastard." It turned out to be the chief of the SD office in Athens. Fackenheim was not much comforted when Müller assured him that the Abwehr would protect him.

As Fackenheim would eventually find out, he had become a pawn in the deadly rivalry between the Abwehr and the SD. At last he got his final instructions, and on the night of October 10, 1941, was taken by Müller to an airport near Athens, where he boarded a German aircraft. A few hours later, he was floating downward beneath a camouflaged parachute toward a vineyard outside Haifa.

Fackenheim had hardly hit the ground when he saw trucks and cars gathered on a nearby road. Troops were yelling instructions to each other. Sirens wailed in the distance. Clearly the British were very much awake and looking for him. Had they seen his parachute?

It was more serious than that. The British had been tipped off to the exact time and place of his arrival—by agents working for the SD. In a move to embarrass the Abwehr, the SD had planted information that the parachutist would not be Herr Koch, but rather a well-known SS general, Obergruppenführer Erich Koch. Such a high-ranking Nazi could only be arriving in Palestine to coordinate a large sabotage operation or lead an Arab revolt. The British were frantic to find the dangerous visitor.

Somehow Fackenheim got out of the vineyard and past a British roadblock to a bus stop. There he melted into the morning rush-hour crowd, boarded a bus, and was soon in downtown Haifa. But British military police were patrolling everywhere, checking identity papers. As a last resort, Fackenheim entered a British command post and told a story of being a Jewish refugee from Germany who had landed from a boat on a Haifa beach the night before. But as soon as the British saw the name, Paul Koch, on his forged papers, they arrested him.

Some of the British counterintelligence officers who questioned Fackenheim concluded that he was exactly what he admitted to being—a low-level spy. But others clung to the notion that he was an SS general. Taken to a military jail outside Cairo, Fackenheim was interrogated relentlessly and threatened with execution. Finally, he was tried by a military court, and was only saved from being shot or hanged by the work of an Irish lawyer assigned to his defense. At the last minute, the lawyer located an elderly Jewish woman in Palestine who testified that she had known Fackenheim and his parents back in Germany. Found not guilty, Fackenheim was interned as an enemy alien. He survived the war, an unlikely prospect had he remained in Dachau, and afterward took up a new profession—writing spy novels.

Paul Fackenheim, an Abwehr agent in Palestine, used a grid to send and receive coded messages. After the British arrested him, he sent his superiors a note that, decoded on the grid, read, *"Bin erwischt. Hoffe weg zu kommen. Koch* (I have been caught. Hope to escape.)." Koch was Fackenheim's code name.

On the eastern front, the Abwehr employed huge numbers of spies—and sent most of them only a few miles behind the Russian lines. Their missions were strictly tactical, intended to inform local Wehrmacht field commanders of the strength and type of Soviet forces that were deployed against them. The Germans had virtually no agents in Moscow or other Russian cities—an intelligence vacuum that caused Hitler and the high command to consistently underestimate the Red Army's strength and resolve.

The Abwehr's failure to have espionage networks in place in the Soviet Union was doubtless caused in part by the difficulty of lodging spies in a totalitarian society. But it probably also reflected an ingrained prejudice. Few top Abwehr officers believed in Hitler's racial theories, but many shared the long-standing German prejudice that the Slavs were an inferior people, hardly worth spying on.

Under a plan code-named Walli I, the Abwehr assigned to each German army special spy units with so-called front agents, or line crossers. And the agents did just that, crossing the front lines into Russian-held territory to a depth of a dozen miles at most and returning a day or two later to report on whatever military activity they had seen.

The agents were briefed beforehand about the area they were to enter and what to look for. To get them safely through the lines, each Abwehr unit had specialists called *Schleusenderen* (literally, "sluicers"), who picked the right spots to insert the spies—parts of the front without trench systems, barbed wire, mines, and other perils.

There were other sorts of spies as well, so-called deep agents who penetrated up to 200 miles behind the lines to look for enemy troop concentrations and the movements of supplies. These agents were usually parachuted in, stayed longer, reported by radio, and were often flown out by small planes touching down in empty rear areas—if they got out at all. For both types of spies the attrition rate was enormous. Hundreds were caught and summarily executed. In an eleven-month period, one Abwehr command dispatched no fewer than 150 teams of between three and ten agents each. Members of only two teams returned safely. A few agents, though, led charmed lives. One woman, named Sonia, the daughter of a Russian nobleman, parachuted seven times on deep missions and came back every time.

Three German military intelligence experts (*far left and seated*) on the eastern front question Soviet prisoners of war—prime sources of information on the strength, position, and intentions of the Russian forces.

A German map compiled from intelligence sources pinpoints Soviet mineral reserves in vivid colors: coal in red, chromium in yellow, iron in green, and manganese in blue. Derricks symbolize oil fields.

The Germans had one Soviet superspy. This was a celebrated mole known only as Max who was located in Moscow and, to judge by his reports, had entrée to the highest councils in the Soviet Union. Max's messages, which he sent out almost daily, always contained some useful tidbit of information, and occasionally he produced blockbusters. In mid-1942, for example, he reported the Soviet high command's decision to let the German armies advance, trading land for time. Later that year, he reported with considerable accuracy on a war council in the Kremlin at which Stalin and his top generals planned the winter offensive that doomed 250,000 German soldiers at Stalingrad—a warning that was ignored at huge cost by Hitler.

But who Max was and how he operated was a mystery. All Canaris knew was that Max's reports came by radio and were passed on to Abwehr headquarters by a Viennese named Fritz Kauders. Some thought Max must be a doctor who attended Kremlin higher-ups, including perhaps even Stalin himself. Others thought he might be someone who had managed to tap the Kremlin phone lines, or had connections with Japanese intelligence, which had operatives in Moscow. Skeptics suspected he was a Soviet double agent, passing on information of dubious worth. Or perhaps Max had simply been invented by Kauders for his own profit. The truth of the matter may never be known. ✚

As seen from a clock tower, wartime Cairo, a fertile ground for espionage, rises behind two centuries-old mosques.

A Clandestine Gambit Called Condor

Cairo in 1942 was a political and ethnic melting pot boiling with intrigue, Egyptian nationalism, and fierce anti-British sentiment. It was also center stage for Operation Condor, one of the most colorful and dangerous spy dramas of the war.

At the core of this daring plot was a charming and sophisticated playboy named John Eppler, whose exotic background fitted him for such a role. Eppler was born in 1914 to German parents living in Alexandria. After his father died, Eppler's mother married Saleh Gaafer, a wealthy pro-British Egyptian lawyer who adopted Eppler, raised him as a Muslim, and changed his name to Hussein Gaafer.

Eppler's German roots, his knowledge of Arabic language and customs, and the expensive education provided by his stepfather made him a nearly perfect candidate for the life of a spy. Approached by Nazi recruiters in 1938, Eppler embraced his German heritage and launched an espionage career that included exploits in Turkey, Lebanon, Iraq, and Afghanistan before embarking on Operation Condor.

In the spring of 1942, Rommel was preparing for his advance into Egypt, and he desperately needed an agent inside the country to report on British troop strength, morale, and plans for the defensive. Eppler was an obvious choice, but how could he get into Cairo? Alexandria, at the mouth of the Nile, was a sealed port, and entry by river seemed too risky. So did another alternative—arrival by parachute. An overland approach, through the desert, was judged to be the surest bet. In May 1942, Eppler and a small band of German commandos set out from a remote oasis in the Western Desert, bound for Cairo—1,000 miles away across the trackless dunes.

Four-year-old John Eppler and his mother pose with their Sudanese houseboys in the garden of their villa in Alexandria in 1918. Later, Eppler's reputation as a frivolous, over-indulged playboy served him well as a cover for espionage.

Eppler wears Arab garb for a spy mission to Afghanistan in 1939. Eppler, chameleon-like, could adopt whatever look a particular clandestine venture required.

After a difficult three-week trek, Eppler's party arrived at their destination near the Nile River. The

Radio operator Peter Monkaster *(left)* relaxes with Eppler before leaving on the grueling desert trek to Cairo. Monkaster carried an American passport obtained for him by German agents in the United States.

خطر
الطريق في المنزل وعر وذو منعطفات
**DANGEROUS DESCENT
DRIVE IN BOTTOM GEAR**

Count Ladislaus de Almaszy, a Hungarian-born explorer and an expert on the Western Desert, served as guide for Eppler's party. Here he pauses beneath a bilingual sign near British lines.

spy, disguised as a stranded British officer, was accompanied by his radio operator, a German from East Africa named Peter Monkaster, who posed as an American friend. The two continued alone on foot to a British outpost where they were given gin fizzes, lunch, and a lift to the train that would take them into Cairo. After sending a signal to Rommel that they had arrived safely, Eppler and Monkaster, lavishly funded by the German intelligence service, set up headquarters on a Nile houseboat and went about the business of building their cover as two wealthy and dissolute young men about town.

The terrace of Shepheard's Hotel teems with an international clientele, including many British officers. This bar, Eppler's first stop upon reaching Cairo, was one of many that the spy visited nightly to pick up information.

Hekmat (*opposite*) plies her trade at a Cairo nightclub. Even the jaded Eppler was not immune to her charms. "Certainly she was a terrible strumpet," he wrote, "and could conquer any man."

Hekmat Fahmy entertains a British captain and his New Zealander friend. Nights like this often ended on her houseboat—adjacent to Eppler's—where she would smoothly extract military information from besotted, unwary officers.

The Fateful Persuasions of a Dancer

Of all his contacts in Cairo, none served Eppler better than the seductive dancer Hekmat Fahmy, an expert at prying secret information from the British. "An Englishman who has just made love to you," she once told an interrogator, "not only trusts you—he can't stop talking."

One of those loose-tongued Eng-lishmen was a major assigned to deliver an important dispatch to British headquarters in the desert. Before leaving on his mission, how-ever, the major stopped for one last rendezvous with Hekmat. After he foolishly revealed the purpose of his trip into the desert, Hekmat gave him a drugged cocktail and handed the dispatch case over to Eppler. The papers, marked "Most Secret," contained unit-by-unit British plans for defending the city against Rommel's anticipated attack. It was exactly what Eppler had been look-ing for in the weeks since he arrived in Cairo. Success, it seemed, was only a radio dispatch away.

Debacle on a Nile River Houseboat

Eppler's mission ended badly. Frustrated by a radio failure that kept their messages from Rommel, Eppler and Monkaster drank themselves into a stupor on their houseboat. Authorities, tipped off by an informant and led by Major A. W. Sansom, raided the boat and arrested the pair without firing a shot. To make matters worse for the Germans, Sansom's officers cracked Eppler's code and used it to transmit false information to Rommel. That deception is said to have played a part in Rommel's defeat at the battle of El Alamein.

Major A. W. Sansom (*opposite*) spoke all dialects of Arabic and had operatives throughout Cairo. He and Eppler—each unaware of the other's identity—once shared a bottle of champagne at the Kit Kat Cabaret.

Peter Monkaster strikes a jaunty pose in a Cairo prison camp. He slashed his throat while awaiting interrogation, but was saved by orderlies who rushed him to a hospital. Like Eppler, he was released after the war.

A dapper John Eppler, saved from a firing squad by his stepfather's influential British friends, seems completely at ease in prison camp. After the war, he moved to Europe and became a millionaire businessman.

Eppler and Monkaster, living on a houseboat in Cairo's fashionable Zamalek district (*below*), were popular with their neighbors—including a British major who unwittingly helped them install a high-powered aerial for their hidden radio.

Focusing
on the
Enemy

In 1930, a young German aviator named Theodor Rowehl, acting entirely on his own, chartered a plane and used a powerful new camera to take high-altitude photographs of Polish fortifications near the German border. When he showed the remarkably detailed pictures to German intelligence officers, his career in aerial reconnaissance was launched.

Starting out with a single Junkers W 34 (which in 1929 set the world altitude record of 41,800 feet), Rowehl eventually commanded a corps of 300 crack pilots, about fifty special high-altitude planes, and some of the most sophisticated aerial photography equipment in the world. Between 1934 and 1943, Rowehl's elite Luftwaffe reconnaissance group took millions of secret photographs, including, in his words, pictures of "every blade of grass between Lincolnshire and Portsmouth" in England, as well as of vital strategic points in nearly every other theater of the war.

The ability of Rowehl's pilots to climb far above the ceiling of enemy fighter planes and anti-aircraft guns allowed them to work virtually without risk. Observing the enemy aircraft circling miles below "was like looking down into an aquarium," German pilot Siegfried Knemeyer recalled, "and seeing the fishes swimming."

Colonel Theodor Rowehl, a former World War I reconnaissance pilot, began his high-altitude spy missions as a private citizen working for the Abwehr. In 1938, one of his planes took a picture of Leningrad and its Neva River *(opposite)* while flying out of sight at about 25,000 feet.

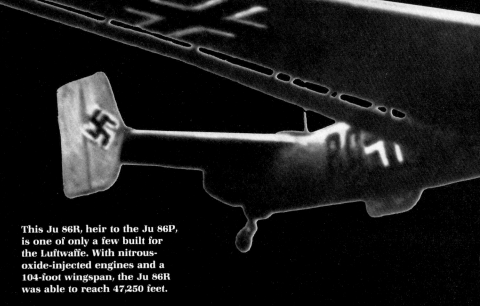

A Highflying Aircraft for Observation

Although Colonel Rowehl's squadron flew a variety of aircraft, by far the most effective was the specially modified Junkers 86P. Rebuilt from the airframe of an obsolete bomber and transport craft called the Ju 86, this twin-engine, low-wing monoplane had a ceiling of 42,000 feet and a range of 1,600 miles. The crew and cameras were housed in a heated, pressurized "egg" in the nose of the craft.

The camera usually carried by the Ju 86P was the Zeiss Rb 30, which stood nearly three feet tall and weighed more than 160 pounds with all its accessories and a full load of film (almost 200 feet). It was the power of the camera's telescopic lenses that enabled the crew to take sharp, detailed photos from a safe altitude.

In the first years of the war, Rowehl's Ju 86Ps were virtually untouchable. Not until August of 1942 did the Allies manage to shoot down one of the German planes. By 1944, however, the picture had changed. The altitude ceilings of Allied fighters had greatly increased, making the slow-flying, unarmed spy planes much more vulnerable.

This Ju 86R, heir to the Ju 86P, is one of only a few built for the Luftwaffe. With nitrous-oxide-injected engines and a 104-foot wingspan, the Ju 86R was able to reach 47,250 feet.

A Ju 86P reconnaissance crew goes over the details of an upcoming mission with German intelligence officers *(in civilian dress)*. In the background, an He 116, another plane frequently used in spy work, waits its turn.

A crewman enters this Junkers 86P through a porthole that was sealed before takeoff to maintain cabin pressure at extreme altitudes. The Ju 86P was the first military aircraft to possess a pressurized cabin.

This Zeiss Rb 30 camera was fitted with a 75-cm (29.5-inch) telephoto lens capable of recording surface details clearly and precisely from seven miles up.

The ventral camera ports on this Junkers 86P-2 were aligned to take overlapping pictures of the target on the ground.

An Aerial View of the Rock

A German photo interpreter gets the quickest possible intelligence by reading wet negatives while they are still in the film cassette.

In 1940, when Hitler began plotting to capture Gibraltar in the western Mediterranean, that peninsula fortress was so heavily defended against infiltration that airborne reconnaissance was the primary source of preinvasion intelligence. The plan was eventually abandoned, but not before a detailed mapping of the strategic bastion had been undertaken.

To cope with the ever-changing battlefield situations encountered in the blitzkriegs of Poland and France—and those anticipated on Gibraltar—the Germans had learned to extract information instantly from reconnaissance photography. Unlike the British, who waited for prints to be made from the exposed film, Luftwaffe photo readers learned to make their first analysis from negatives placed on viewing screens. Later, prints were made, and intelligence officers pored over them to analyze their content in greater detail.

To save precious time, these German photo technicians in North Africa work on location, using the desert sun to dry the film on rollers. Each of the negatives measured one foot square.

This reconnaissance photo of Gibraltar shows the southern tip of the Rock and Gibraltar Harbor. The arrows, made by the photoanalyst, indicate the locations of Allied warships.

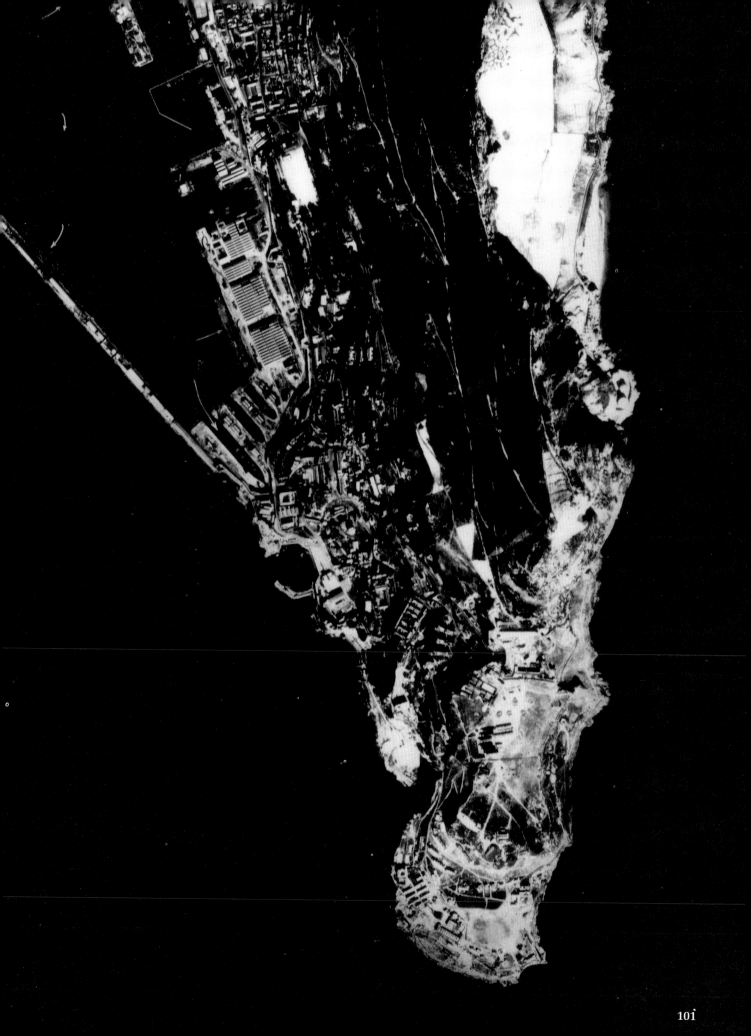

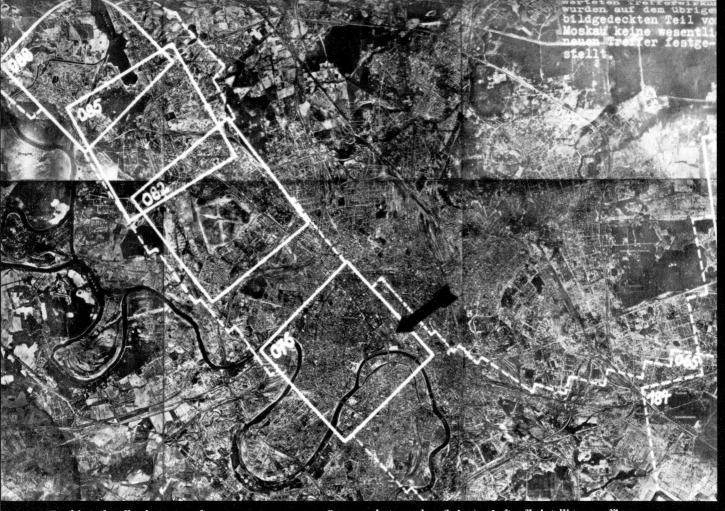

On this Luftwaffe photomap of Moscow and its environs, an arrow in frame 076 pinpoints the Kremlin. Broken lines indicate poorly focused photos.

German photo readers (below) working in Greece in 1941 piece together a large photomosaic that will be used by bombing crews to identify targets.

Luftwaffe intelligence officers inspect aerial photo negatives in a light box to identify potential bombing targets, such as enemy defenses or supply depots.

Missions of Delicacy and Daring

As the war continued, photo readers working for the Luftwaffe began putting together the detailed photomaps and -mosaics necessary for long-range planning. Collecting the material for this kind of photo interpretation required almost superhuman skills on the part of Rowehl's pilots.

Because of the narrow field of vision inherent in cameras with such long focal lengths, a slight lift of a wing or a minute shift off course could mean the failure of a mission. Photo interpreters needed a 60 percent overlap between consecutive photos to make accurate maps and mosaics. If the plane was not flying level, the overlap could drop to under 10 percent or increase to 90 percent. In addition, the pilot had to be aware of the angle of the sun and the lines of approach to the objective—and still protect himself and his crew from the enemy. Because they had to meet such extraordinarily exacting standards, the men who flew reconnaissance planes were considered some of the finest pilots in the war.

German notations on this photo indicate Allied supplies stockpiled on a beach *(upper right)* in Iran, awaiting shipment across the Caspian Sea to Russia.

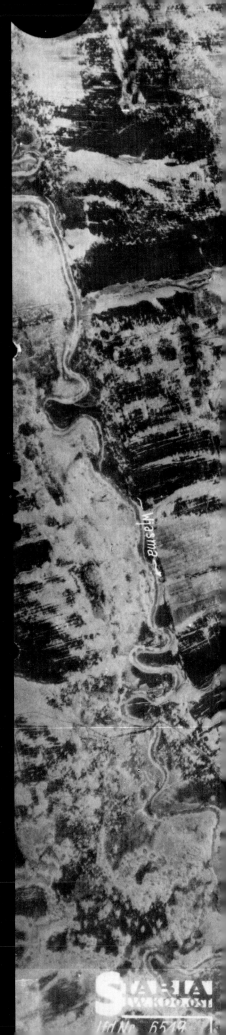

A Clear Picture of Destruction

Perhaps the most dangerous aerial reconnaissance missions were flights to assess the damage done by Luftwaffe bombing raids. Bomber crews could not be expected to gauge the results of their attacks— or even to know whether their missiles had hit the target. So it fell to reconnaissance pilots to make follow-up flights and obtain the crucial information. To get an accurate picture of bomb craters, wrecked buildings, collapsed bridges, and other damage, the pilots often had to fly at much lower altitudes than usual. This made them much more vulnerable to Allied fighter planes and antiaircraft fire from the ground. Adding to the hazard, Allied defenders came to expect the assessment flights on the heels of bombing raids and were well prepared to intercept the German spy planes.

A Luftwaffe cameraman peers through a viewfinder while his pilot keeps an eye out for flak during a mission to photograph the results of a bombing raid.

The circular notations on this photograph pinpoint damage done by Luftwaffe bombs to a railroad line near the city of Vyazma in the Soviet Union.

Kakarewo

○——= Große Sprengung
— — —= Kleine   "   "

Sprengst. Bahnl. 5 Km N Wjasma

SU **S.P.3-166**
M. etwa 1 : 14 000

105

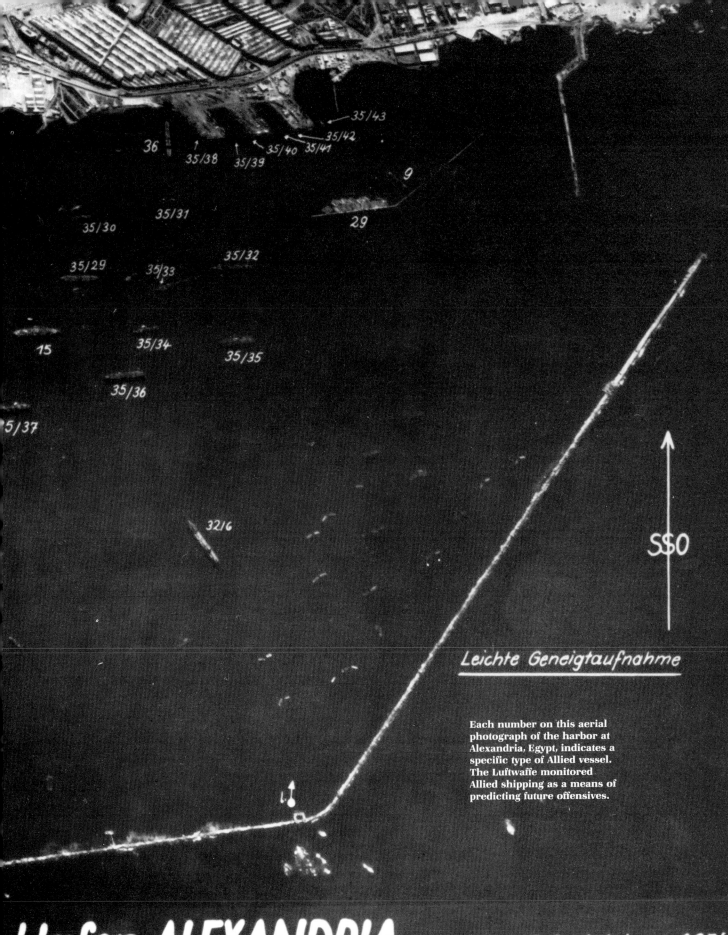

Each number on this aerial
photograph of the harbor at
Alexandria, Egypt, indicates a
specific type of Allied vessel.
The Luftwaffe monitored
Allied shipping as a means of
predicting future offensives.

Leichte Geneigtaufnahme

SSO

Hafen ALEXANDRIA

Aufgen. am 28.1.44, 09³⁵ Uhr

Karte Ägypten 1:100 000 Blatt Alexandria

Maßstab etwa 1:15800

Beob. Lt. Effenberger

2.-(F) 123

107

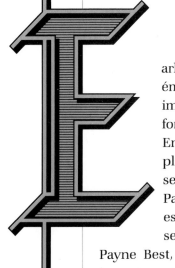

THREE

The War against Spies

Early in September 1939, soon after the outbreak of war, a German émigré named Franz Fischer approached Britain's two most important spies in the Netherlands. A group of generals had formed a conspiracy to overthrow Hitler, he said. Would the Englishmen be interested in meeting a representative of the plotters? The two agents replied that indeed they would. The senior man was Major R. Henry Stevens, who, from His Majesty's Passport Control Office in The Hague, directed the extensive espionage ring established inside Germany by MI-6, the British secret intelligence service. Stevens's associate was Captain S. Payne Best, a longtime resident of the Netherlands who operated an import-export business as a front for his real work. Stevens and Best already had heard reports of disaffection among the German high command. They hoped to make contact with the conspirators through Fischer and then assist in the coup against Hitler.

What the Britishers did not know was that Fischer was himself a spy—Agent F479 of the Sicherheitsdienst, or SD, the German security service. The officer they were to meet, one Captain Schaemmel, was also an agent—Major Walter Schellenberg, the fast-rising young chief of counterespionage for the Gestapo. The entire affair was a ruse to elicit from the British any information they might have about actual military plots against the Führer.

To perfect his role in the masquerade, Schellenberg immersed himself in the identity of the man whose name he had appropriated. He took up residence in Düsseldorf, where the real Schaemmel was based as a transportation officer with the armed forces high command, and proceeded to observe his behavior and appearance and study detailed reports on his background. On October 21, feeling comfortable in his guise, Schellenberg drove to the Netherlands for the first of his meetings with the British agents. He quickly succeeded in winning their confidence and earnestly told them the generals needed assurances that London would deal fairly with the post-Nazi regime they planned.

At the next session, Schellenberg arrived in the company of an older man

The menacing shadow of an enemy agent looms large on a wall poster urging silence on the German public—a warning backed by pervasive police surveillance and tight border controls.

whom he introduced as Captain Hausmann—"the right hand of the leader of our opposition group." Hausmann actually was his old friend Max de Crinis, a Berlin University psychiatrist, elegant, highly intelligent, and cultured—altogether convincing as a general's aide-de-camp. The four dined at Best's home in The Hague, talked of music and painting, and enjoyed what Schellenberg described as the most marvelous oysters he had ever tasted. The next morning, at the offices of Best's business cover, the Continental Trading Corporation, the British obligingly gave Schellenberg a radio set and a code that would enable him to communicate with them.

Negotiations proceeded apace. By early November, Schellenberg had made tentative arrangements with the British to fly to London with one of the purported plotters. He had already selected a German industrialist and devoted Nazi to play the role of the dissident general who led the plotters. He planned to introduce him to Best and Stevens at their next rendezvous, on November 9 at a café in the little Dutch border town of Venlo.

But the night before the meeting, Schellenberg's scheme took a bizarre turn. Shortly after midnight, Heinrich Himmler, chief of the SS and the RSHA, the Reich's security apparatus, telephoned in a fury with the news that Hitler had narrowly escaped assassination in Munich. The Führer had delivered an address marking the anniversary of the 1923 Beer Hall Putsch and had left the building minutes before a bomb exploded behind the speakers' platform, killing seven people. "There's no doubt the British secret service is behind it all," raged Himmler. "When you meet the British agents for your conference tomorrow, you are to arrest them immediately and bring them to Germany."

The next afternoon, when Best and Stevens arrived for their rendezvous in Venlo, three Gestapo cars were positioned, engines idling, just across the border. As the Buick containing the British agents approached the café where Schellenberg was sipping coffee, one of the Gestapo cars suddenly roared to life. The German vehicle crashed through the frontier barrier and, with its occupants firing submachine guns to pin down the Dutch border guards, raced up to the Buick. The SS men hauled out the two British agents "like bundles of hay," reported Schellenberg with relish, handcuffed them, and dumped them into the open car. Then, tires screaming, the Germans raced in reverse down the street and backward across the border.

The dramatic Venlo affair marked the wartime debut of German efforts in counterintelligence, and while it failed to achieve its information-gathering goal, it provided considerable benefit to the Reich. For one thing, the incident put two key British agents in prison (where they remained for the duration of the war), thereby paralyzing the British espionage network inside Germany. For another, it gave Hitler a convenient scapegoat on

Situated near the German border, this small hotel in the Dutch town of Venlo was the scene of the kidnapping of British MI-6 agents R. Henry Stevens (*near right*) and S. Payne Best in 1939. Spirited off to Germany by the Gestapo, the two spent the war years in a concentration camp.

which to blame the assassination attempt. (The true would-be assassin was a German cabinetmaker named Georg Elser, who was quickly tracked down and imprisoned.) Indeed, six months later, the Führer cited the Venlo incident as provocation for Germany's invasion of the Netherlands. The Dutch, he said, had already violated their own neutrality by allowing British agents to operate on their soil.

After its auspicious start at Venlo, the counterespionage apparatus grew to become perhaps the most effective of all German intelligence operations. The very thought of spies and traitors within the sacred confines of the Third Reich infuriated Hitler, and he meant to ferret them out of the conquered lands as well. Nothing was spared in the effort, from penetrating spy networks and resistance groups to staging elaborate charades such as Schellenberg's caper in the Netherlands. And yet, as was characteristic of Nazi government, the counterintelligence campaign was hampered by a continuing power struggle between contending agencies. In this case, the rivals were the high command's Abwehr—with its Section IIIF counterespionage branch—and the quasi-political ministries gathered under the banner of Himmler's Reich Central Security Office

(RSHA); these included the SD, or Security Service, the SIPO, or Security Police, and the Gestapo, or Secret State Police. The waters were muddied still further by the overlapping—and sometimes conflicting—efforts of a host of organizations that eavesdropped on the enemy, tapping telephones, intercepting radio signals, and breaking codes to discover battle plans and espionage plots.

Aside from indigenous resistance movements, the chief foe was the new British secret service known as the Special Operations Executive (SOE), which was established in 1940 to carry on clandestine warfare behind enemy lines. To occupied France alone during the next four years, the SOE would dispatch nearly 400 agents. A primary German objective would be to subvert or otherwise unravel the networks the SOE established.

The most celebrated Abwehr agent in France, Sergeant Hugo Bleicher,

defined counterintelligence as "the art of detecting and exploiting the secret operations of the enemy." His job, he wrote, was "to discover enemy espionage, so to speak, without uncovering it." A former clerk in a Hamburg export firm, Bleicher was in his forties, with a sincere face and horn-rimmed spectacles that lent him an owlish appearance. He spoke excellent French and often posed as a "Monsieur Jean" when contacting enemy networks. He also had a French girlfriend to advise him about her countrymen and, as he wrote, serve as a "guide to their psychology."

It was Bleicher's persuasiveness with women that brought him success in his first major case. In the autumn of 1941, the Abwehr penetrated a spy ring called Interallié, or the Allied Circle, and a number of agents were arrested. Bleicher was assigned to question one of the captured operatives, Mathilde Carré, an attractive Frenchwoman known to her comrades as La Chatte—the Cat. He conducted the interrogation over a sumptuous dinner in a private suite at one of Paris's finest hotels. That night, the Cat became his lover and a double agent, ostensibly loyal to British intelligence but actually serving Germany.

Under instructions from Bleicher, Carré made contact with a French Resistance organizer named Pierre de Vomécourt, who had lost his radio link with London. Carré led Vomécourt to believe that she could reestablish communications, and he passed her messages for the SOE, which she then turned over to Bleicher. Eventually, the Frenchman became suspicious and confronted Carré, who broke down and confessed her complicity with Bleicher. Taking advantage of her distraught state, Vomécourt did some persuasive talking of his own. Once again the Cat was turned; she became a triple agent. At Vomécourt's behest, she fed her German lover bogus information and then administered the unkindest cut of all. She concocted such a convincing tale about her potential value to him if she were to operate in London that Bleicher, posing as a friendly agent on one of Interallié's old radio transmitters, persuaded the SOE to provide the transportation for her trip across the Channel. And so, on February 26, 1942, the Cat and Vomécourt fled France in a British torpedo boat.

But Bleicher had the last laugh. After Vomécourt was parachuted back into France a few weeks later, Bleicher nabbed him, temporarily leaving the British without an organized network in occupied France. As for the Cat, her dalliance and collaboration with the German agent she now scorned earned her a British prison cell for the duration of the war.

Bleicher went on to other triumphs, but not without some uneasy moments—and not without making enemies in the archrival SD. Early in 1943, he infiltrated a British-run Resistance network by pretending to be Colonel Heinrich, a dissident officer in German intelligence. Like Schel-

Montmartre in Paris sprawls below the wing of a Fieseler Storch aircraft, a type used to trace illicit radios. The district was home to Roman Garby-Czerniawski (*far left*), a Polish officer who ran the Interallié spy ring until he was betrayed in 1941 by an arrested agent; the same sweep netted Mathilde Carré (*near left*), alias La Chatte.

lenberg in the Venlo caper, Bleicher even offered to fly to London to discuss a plot against Hitler. The deception completely fooled the British, and almost brought Bleicher himself to grief when one of their agents was arrested by the SD in Marseilles carrying a glowing written report on the traitorous German colonel. The SD was not in the least amused, and in fact harbored suspicions that Bleicher might have gone over to the enemy. The sergeant had to do some fast explaining before he was cleared.

Bleicher's ploy helped lead to the arrest of two important British agents: Captain Peter Churchill, whom Bleicher at first mistakenly believed to be the nephew of Britain's prime minister, and Odette Sansom, the Frenchwoman whose service would win her high honors from the governments of Britain and France. But once its suspicions were aroused, the SD neither forgot nor forgave. The Colonel Heinrich affair, along with a transparent ambition that alienated many of his superiors in the Abwehr, might have accounted for the fact that Bleicher never rose above the rank of sergeant.

The chief of SD counterespionage in France, Karl Boemelburg, was a crusty old professional who could not be expected to take kindly to the likes of Bleicher. A capable but hard-drinking veteran of the SS in his late fifties, Boemelburg had been rooting out dissidents, spies, and other threats to the Reich since 1931. He so loathed Communists and Jews that, in the garden of his Paris headquarters, he set up a shooting gallery with such targets as portraits of Soviet leaders, French Communists, and caricatures of Jews. Then he would get roaring drunk and blast away with his pistol while his dog—named Stalin—barked furiously.

Among the string of informers and paid agents run by Boemelburg one man stood out: an extraordinary double agent named Henri Déricourt. A Frenchman in his mid-thirties, Déricourt had spent the decade before the war as a civilian pilot, variously flying mail planes and airliners and cultivating a taste for danger. He tested new aircraft and for a while traveled with a troupe of wing-walking aerial acrobats. He also dabbled in espionage. As early as 1936, he flew agents of the Deuxième Bureau, the French intelligence service, on photographic missions over the German border. After the fall of France, American intelligence enlisted him to report on the German aircraft and defenses he observed on his occasional flights to French North Africa. If Déricourt's sense of adventure attracted him to spying, he soon found that he also possessed an operative's natural gifts: charm, self-confidence, and limitless guile.

In late 1942, the British SOE recruited him and trained him in England to serve as a ground liaison officer, managing the arrival and departure of the aircraft—Lysanders and Hudsons—that shuttled agents in and out of northern France. The British parachuted Déricourt back into France in

January 1943, but before beginning work, he renewed his acquaintance with Karl Boemelburg. Déricourt had met Boemelburg in 1938 in Paris, where the German was operating under cover as a spy. Now, as a newly minted British agent code-named Gilbert, he offered his services to Boemelburg—for money and, he asserted, the crusade against communism.

Whatever Déricourt's motives, Boemelburg was delighted to recruit him, and the pair began one of the most productive partnerships of the shadow war. Designated BOE/48—Boemelburg's forty-eighth agent—Déricourt supplied a stream of valuable information to the SD chief. He would notify Boemelburg before every aircraft arrival, and the Germans would be waiting—not to capture the agents but to follow them at a distance. The surveillance teams were made up of French criminals and corrupt former policemen. Their assignment was to trace the agents' movements and contacts to build up a picture of British espionage in northern France. Déricourt added to the mosaic by revealing all he knew about the more than 100 agents who passed through his hands in the coming months.

Déricourt performed another service of inestimable value. Several days before a flight, he would turn over to Boemelburg the bag of outgoing dispatches entrusted to him by SOE agents. Boemelburg would return it to him twenty-four hours later, having had all the letters, sketches of sabotage plans, and other vital intelligence photographed for SD files.

Boemelburg was particularly interested in a new British network in northern France, code-named Prosper. He quickly surmised that the mission of this network was to assist in the eventual Allied invasion of France. Boemelburg deliberately let Prosper blossom into the SOE's largest European operation, with more than 1,000 British and French agents. He was certain that Prosper, via Déricourt, would provide him with a priceless piece of intelligence: the date of the Allied invasion. By June 1943, Boemelburg's reports to Berlin about Prosper and Agent BOE/48 had reached the attention of the Führer himself. If Déricourt could only get that magic date, Boemelburg told his deputy, their careers would be made.

But at this point, the SD's rivals in the Abwehr, jealous of Boemelburg's growing prestige, set out to discredit his double agent. A pair of Abwehr agents from Holland tried to lure Déricourt into a trap they had baited with black-market diamonds. When that failed, Sergeant Hugo Bleicher took the wholly astounding step of betraying Déricourt to the British. Through an informer in another SOE network, Bleicher arranged a meeting with Prosper's leader. Then, in his favorite pose as Colonel Heinrich, disloyal German intelligence officer, Bleicher blatantly denounced Déricourt as a traitor to the Allied cause. More amazing still, the British refused to believe the accusation and made no move against the spy.

In calmer days before the war, pilot Henri Déricourt *(far right)* chats with his radioman beside their mail plane. Déricourt parlayed charm and flying skills into simultaneous jobs with British and German intelligence.

Infuriated by the Abwehr's action and obsessed with learning the invasion date, Boemelburg finally cracked down on Prosper. The network leader, Francis Suttill, was arrested on June 24; by the end of July, the SD had apprehended dozens of British agents and hundreds upon hundreds of French men and women working for the ring. Confronted by the mountain of evidence supplied by Agent BOE/48, Suttill finally confessed a date for the invasion of France—but not the right one, of which he was ignorant. He said that the Allies would land during the first week in September, when in fact the invasion was still ten months off. Suttill thus became one of the many unwitting instruments of a grand British deception code-named Operation Cockade. The aim was to persuade the Germans of an imminent invasion in order to pin down their armies in western Europe and assist the embattled Soviets in the east.

Boemelburg was taken in, but Hitler reasoned differently. The Führer was certain Prosper loomed so large in Allied plans that its collapse would

actually compel the Americans and British to call off the invasion. When September came and went without incident, Boemelburg was relieved of his Paris post and shipped off to Vichy to head the local SD detachment. His bosses in Berlin opted for the approach favored by his deputy, Josef Kieffer, who concentrated on arresting spies rather than trying to outwit them. "I have not been tough enough," Boemelburg told Déricourt during a farewell dinner at the German's mansion in the Paris suburbs.

Four months later, Déricourt also left Paris. Before flying to London with his wife, Jeannot, on the night of February 8, 1944, Déricourt had one more rendezvous with Boemelburg, who handed him two million francs—more than enough for the Frenchman to buy the country estate he yearned for. The British knew nothing of the gift, but they had sufficient reason, including Sergeant Bleicher's avowal, to suspect Déricourt of informing on the Prosper network. Yet Déricourt, cool as always, talked his way out of the charges, and was even recommended for—though not awarded—the Distinguished Service Order (DSO), one of Britain's highest honors.

Karl Boemelburg *(far right)*, **the chief of SD counterespionage in France, relaxes at a sidewalk café in Paris during a meeting with subordinates and a French collaborator.**

Irrepressible, he soon joined up as a pilot for Free French intelligence and narrowly survived when his plane crashed in France on a low-flying reconnaissance mission. The fascinating possibility is that he may well have deserved Britain's DSO. Evidence later suggested that all along he had been a triple agent in the employ of a separate branch of MI-6 and that he had pretended to go over to the Germans in order to play a vital role in the monumental subterfuge of Operation Cockade.

Whatever the truth of these complex intrigues, a melancholy result was evident when the Allies landed on the Normandy beaches in June 1944. As Resistance networks rose up everywhere to assist the liberators, the weakest effort was in northern France, where nearly 1,000 men and women languished in prison because of that enigmatic alliance between Boemelburg and Déricourt.

In the campaigns of cross and double cross, a fundamental technique of German counterespionage was the *Funkspiel,* or radio playback game. The goal of the game was to establish a radio link with the Allies that they would believe originated with their own agent. The *Funkspiel* required the capture of a transmitter and, in most cases, the cooperation of its operator. The Germans then could feed misleading information to the Allies and gain insight into their activities and intentions.

The war's most successful radio game was carried out in the occupied Netherlands under the code name Operation Nordpol, or North Pole. The director of this coup was Major Hermann Giskes, a one-time businessman, now in his mid-forties, with a natural gift for counterespionage. Giskes's exemplary work in Paris after the fall of France had come to the attention of the head of the Abwehr, Admiral Canaris, who posted him to The Hague in the summer of 1941. Giskes proved to be an interrogator of great skill and sensitivity who, as one captured enemy agent remarked in some wonder, "clearly had a sense of humor."

North Pole commenced on March 6, 1942, when the Germans raided an apartment in The Hague and seized a British SOE radio transmitter and its Dutch-born operator, Hubert Lauwers. With friendly persuasion, Giskes talked Lauwers into making another transmission in return for promises of leniency for the family with whom he was hiding. The British agent assumed that his superiors in London would immediately realize that he was in German hands. The tip-off would be the absence of his security check: a prearranged signal required in all regular transmissions to assure London that the operator was safe. The check consisted of a recurring pattern of mistakes—in Lauwers's case, a deliberate spelling error in every sixteenth letter of his enciphered text.

The transmission, six days after his arrest, did not work out as Lauwers intended. London ignored the telltale omission of his security check, just as it disregarded a virtual red flag: the letter groupings *CAU* and *GHT* (spelling the word *caught*) in later transmissions. His SOE superiors evidently could not believe that he would cooperate with the Germans and went ahead with business as usual—to the point of announcing the arrival of another agent, code-named Abor. When Abor, along with containers of weapons, was parachuted onto a remote plain on the night of March 27, German-paid Dutchmen were there to capture him.

All that spring, Giskes raked in a harvest of SOE agents. Most were operatives already in the country who were exposed during the radio game. Others were agents who parachuted into German hands carrying radio transmitters. By summer, Giskes controlled five transmitters and their operators. Fearing that the captured operators might try to sound an alert, Giskes gradually began assigning Germans to handle the transmissions, though it entailed the risk that London would detect a new hand on the Morse key. He knew that each operator had his own "handwriting"—a unique personal rhythm distinguishable to an experienced ear. At first, he took the precaution of telling London that a reserve operator from the Dutch underground was filling in. But this proved unnecessary: London had neglected to make a recording of each operator's handwriting and could not tell the difference.

Agents and weapons containers kept floating out of the sky into the arms of German reception committees. In all, Giskes arranged nearly 200 air-drops and collected an arsenal of weapons, including 8,000 small arms, 300 machine guns, 2,000 hand grenades, and more than 16 tons of explosives. Moreover, Luftwaffe fighter planes alerted by Giskes shot down a dozen four-engined British bombers after they had disgorged their cargo of agents and matériel. North Pole was going so well, Giskes later noted, that while the British believed every fairy tale he concocted, his own superiors in Berlin at first found it hard to accept his amazing reports.

Giskes devised ever more resourceful stratagems. When London sent orders to destroy a towering radio mast used by the German navy to communicate with its U-boats, he staged a mock raid with blank cartridges—and then radioed the SOE a graphic and sorrowful account of the raid's failure. Much to Giskes's amusement, London radioed back that one of the agents who supposedly took part in the bogus attack had been awarded a medal for valor. To give a further appearance of Resistance activity and mask the collapse of the Dutch underground, Giskes arranged for a spectacular afternoon show in the middle of the Meuse River in Rotterdam. He had his men blow up an old canal barge laden with scrap metal—

Major Hermann Giskes *(above)* **masterminded the Abwehr's Operation North Pole in Holland, sending false information to London and luring dozens of agents into German hands. Giskes's first pawn was SOE agent Hubert Lauwers** *(right),* **a former journalist who was arrested four months after parachuting into Holland.**

while hundreds of Dutch civilians stood on the banks wildly applauding this courageous act of sabotage.

By the summer of 1943, the Germans had captured more than fifty Dutch and British agents, arrested hundreds of Resistance workers, and were operating fourteen radio transmitters. Operation North Pole was deemed such a success that Himmler's SIPO, which had cooperated with Giskes and the Abwehr in the operation, tried to grab all the credit. To celebrate "their" triumph, the Security Police threw a lavish party, complete with cash bonuses—and pointedly failed to invite a single Abwehr officer, not even Giskes. But this small perfidy paled beside the subsequent treachery of Himmler's minions, who executed forty-seven of the captured agents at the Mauthausen concentration camp in Austria in 1944. Giskes wrote bitterly that he had turned over the prisoners to Himmler's security men only after their physical safety had been guaranteed to him "formally and in writing."

By then, North Pole had run its course. In August 1943, a pair of captured agents escaped from the one-time theological seminary where they were being held in suburban Haaren and eventually found their way back to England to blow the whistle on Giskes's operation. Giskes tried to discredit their stories, and he almost succeeded with a warning to London that the pair had been "turned around by the Gestapo." He continued to play

A German reception committee celebrates the seizure of an SOE weapons drop into Holland. The delivery, which fell into a forest clearing in early 1944, included crates of ammunition and explosives *(upper left)* and canisters of rifles and machine guns *(lower left)*, all intended for the Dutch Resistance. A Dutch collaborator *(above, far right)* stands by as the cache is loaded onto a trailer by a soldier with grenades tucked in his boots.

the radio hoax, but the stream of agents and weapons drops dried up.

On April 1, 1944—April Fools' Day—Giskes brought Operation North Pole to a formal end after two years and 1,700 messages. In his final transmission to London, the Abwehr officer made a wryly oblique reference to the invasion everyone knew was coming. "We understand that you have been endeavoring for some time to do business in Holland without our assistance," he radioed. "We regret this the more since we have acted for so long as your sole representatives in this country, to our mutual satisfaction. Nevertheless we can assure you that, should you be thinking of paying us

Dutch civilians mill around a burning German military car demolished by a bomb on an Amsterdam street. The Germans sometimes staged similar acts of sabotage to convince British intelligence that smuggled arms were being put to good use.

a visit on the Continent on any extensive scale, we shall give your emissaries the same attention as we have hitherto, and a similarly warm welcome."

In addition to the traditional tools of counterespionage, the Germans relied heavily on the growing technology of communications intelligence. From embryonic beginnings in the First World War, the new instruments for eavesdropping on the enemy were becoming one of the most effective weapons of the hidden war. Like the Allies, German sleuths tapped telephones, tuned in on enemy radio traffic, and intercepted telegraphic messages. They also had considerable success deciphering enemy codes, although none of their achievements matched the extraordinary British feat of cracking the Germans' Enigma cipher *(pages 138-147)*.

Nearly a dozen different agencies of the Reich were involved in the electronic effort. The specialized needs of the military services accounted for part of the proliferation. But pure lust for power also had its effect; many of Hitler's paladins insisted on their own signals establishments even though they all tended to produce similar intelligence. But Hitler approved of the duplication; competition assured a prodigious stream of information while preventing anyone from controlling it.

Among the rival agencies were those of Foreign Minister Joachim von Ribbentrop and Reich Marshal Hermann Göring. Ribbentrop's snoopers listened in on the radio traffic of foreign missions and managed to crack the diplomatic codes of no fewer than thirty-four nations, including those of Germany's Axis partners Italy and Japan. When the Italian foreign minister, Galeazzo Ciano, eventually learned that the Germans were reading his mail, he snorted, "This is good to know. In the future, they will also read what I want them to read."

Göring's personal signals bureau, the Forschungsamt, or Research Office, was both the largest and the most secret of the communications intelligence agencies. An astonishing 6,000 employees listened round-the-clock to telephone conversations, opened mail, intercepted radio and telegraphic communications, and monitored the foreign press. Göring's telephone-tapping web linked 1,000 taps in the Reich and reached into the occupied countries as well. Whenever a call passed through a tapped line, a bulb lit up in a local listening station. A monitor known as a Z-man took notes or wire-recorded the conversation, a summary of which was then forwarded to Berlin by teleprinter for evaluation. The Research Office was particularly interested in economic information; the data benefited Göring both as Germany's economic czar and as Luftwaffe chief seeking targets to bomb.

All the top Nazis schemed to take over their rivals' signals operations. Göring longed to incorporate into his Research Office the ace code breakers in Chi, the ciphers branch of the armed forces high command. Himmler wanted Göring's Research Office folded into his own Reich security apparatus, RSHA, and when he was rebuffed, started his own section of cryptanalysts. Ribbentrop was so envious of the Research Office, and so aggrieved at its meddling in diplomatic affairs, that he sometimes had its intelligence reports retyped on Foreign Ministry paper and stamped to indicate that they had originated with his department.

One of the more impressive technical coups was pulled off by the German Post Office's Forschungsstelle, or Research Institute. Since the Post Office ran the nation's telephone system, its researchers focused on developing equipment to decode the Allies' electronically scrambled telephone conversations. In March 1942, a Forschungsstelle listening post in occupied Holland plucked from the airwaves a transatlantic radiotelephonic conversation between the United States and England and managed to unscramble it. From then on, the station listened in on as many as sixty conversations a day, some of them between Roosevelt and Churchill. But the Allies suspected that the phone link was insecure, and the Germans, for all their superior technology, learned little of real importance.

German monitors and code breakers were more effective out in the field, where they were the single most important source of enemy information. The Luftwaffe's radio intelligence service often provided advance warning of Allied bombing raids, notably on the morning of August 1, 1943, when 178 American bombers took off from Libya bound for the Rumanian oil fields at Ploesti. Soon after they were airborne, a Luftwaffe listening post in Greece intercepted and quickly decoded an American radio message about the impending attack. The alert went out to all air defenses within striking distance of Libya. The antiaircraft guns ringing Ploesti were ready when the Americans roared in over the wells and refineries. The flak, the worst encountered by United States bombers during the entire war, brought down 53 of the aircraft, nearly one-third of the strike force.

In North Africa, General Erwin Rommel won the sobriquet Desert Fox at least partly because of the extraordinary insights he gained through electronic intelligence. Rommel's right arm was the armed forces' Chi ciphers branch. In the autumn of 1941, Chi broke the so-called Black Code, which the Americans used to encrypt reports from military attachés stationed in United States embassies around the world. Rommel and his officers read with fascination the messages of one Colonel Bonner Fellers, the United States military attaché in Cairo. That conscientious officer was determined to learn the lessons of desert warfare and teach them to Washington. He toured the battlefields, quizzed British commanders, and sent home lengthy radiograms. In Germany, a Chi intercept station near Nuremberg

An American B-24 Liberator swoops low over a refinery in Rumania's Ploesti oil fields during a raid on August 1, 1943. Warned of the impending attack by a Luftwaffe code breaker, German antiaircraft defenders knocked out a third of the attacking bomber force.

plucked the Morse dots and dashes from the air and sent them to Berlin headquarters. Chi cryptanalysts converted these Black Code ciphers into plaintext, which was then flashed to Rommel in the desert.

The information, which often reached Rommel only a few hours after the original Cairo transmission, was critical to the Afrikakorps's spectacular drive on Egypt early in 1942. What Rommel delightedly referred to as his "little Fellers" told him precisely how many British tanks were operational and how the British rated their fighting efficiency. In May, when his Afrikakorps actually struck into Egypt, the intercepted American messages pinpointed where the British planned to anchor their defense line and then told Rommel when they changed their mind. One evening late in June, with Rommel practically at the gates of Alexandria, Hitler expressed to colleagues after dinner his hope that "the American in Cairo" would continue to inform them so well.

At about this time, however, Rommel's source dried up. Two German

radiomen taken prisoner by the British gave away the secret. British intelligence, which had itself broken the Black Code, tuned in on Fellers's wireless reports for ten days and found them, someone noted later, "long, detailed, and extremely pessimistic." The British notified the Americans, who scrapped the code and transferred Fellers home. The colonel never knew that he had unwittingly aided the enemy, and in fact received the Distinguished Service Medal for his work in Cairo. "His reports to the War Department," read the citation, "were models of clarity and accuracy." Rommel, who now had to fight without them, surely would have agreed.

For their continuing impact on the war, the German navy's code breakers stood head and shoulders above the rest. This branch—commonly called B-Dienst, short for Beobachtungs-Dienst, or Observation Service—spotlighted the cryptography of Wilhelm Tranow, a civilian of uncommon energy and talent. Tranow had broken his first code as a young naval radioman aboard a battleship in 1914; it happened to be the German navy's own cipher. After the war, Tranow joined what was to become B-Dienst, where he specialized in the ciphers of the Royal Navy until by the time war broke out, he could read the British admiralty's major codes. Tranow had tamed even the daunting British naval cipher, a four-digit code with so-called superencipherment, which was a cipher superimposed atop the code to render it harder to break.

The war was scarcely two weeks old when Tranow and his team claimed their first victim. A German submarine, U-31, acting on information gleaned from a British radio message, sank the steamer *Aviemore* in the Bristol Channel. And in the years that followed, B-Dienst made an indelible mark on the undersea war. The British kept changing their codes, and B-Dienst kept cracking them—and kept expanding to meet the challenge of the burgeoning Allied supply effort across the Atlantic. At its peak, in 1943, B-Dienst operated no fewer than forty-four radio-intercept and direction-finding stations strung from the northern tip of Norway to southern France. These stations logged an average of 8,500 intercepts a day and transmitted them to B-Dienst's Berlin headquarters. There, in the British section alone, nearly 1,000 analysts and clerks, working with automatic sorting and tabulating machines, transformed the ciphers into the convoy information the navy's prowling wolf packs fed upon.

Reports from B-Dienst in early March 1943 set the stage for one of the climactic encounters in the Battle of the Atlantic. Tranow's analysts learned that two huge convoys had sailed from New York Harbor, and the U-boats went after them. When the convoys detected the wolf packs and changed course to avoid them, B-Dienst intercepted the messages and alerted the U-boats. In the resulting three-day battle, German submarines sank twenty-one ships and lost only one of their own. It was the wolf packs' and B-Dienst's greatest success. After that, the tide slowly turned. The Allies employed more escort vessels and better radar, stepped up their own code-breaking efforts, and introduced increasingly complex codes that left even Tranow and B-Dienst straining to keep up.

New technology as well as plain old-fashioned police work figured in a case that unfolded early in the war and remained the greatest triumph of German counterintelligence. The case involved a Soviet spy ring; initial clues to its existence were provided by recently developed direction-finding devices that helped locate clandestine shortwave radio transmitters. Abwehr agents called these secret transmitters pianos, and a network of related transmitters an orchestra. This particular ring became known to German operatives as the Rote Kapelle, or Red Orchestra. Established by the Soviet Union during the late 1930s, the Red Orchestra so permeated western Europe that it reached into the very heart of the Reich itself.

German radio-intercept stations first tuned in to the Red Orchestra early on the morning of June 26, 1941, four days after the invasion of the Soviet Union. The station at Cranz on the Baltic coast picked up a coded message from a transmitter with the call sign *PTX*, which proved to be located in Belgium. A few nights later, signals were intercepted from what turned out to be three different transmitters in Berlin. The broadcasts could only be beamed at Moscow. But the cipher defied the best efforts of the code breakers, and the search for the radios themselves was slowed by the internecine squabbling that so often afflicted German counterespionage.

The Luftwaffe, which possessed the most powerful direction-finding equipment, at first refused to lend it to the Funkabwehr, the signals security unit of the armed forces high command. Only after much negotiation were Luftwaffe detachments with portable gear allowed to join the search in Berlin. The radio sleuths drove unmarked vehicles, wore the uniforms of telephone mechanics, and worked their equipment concealed by the street shelters ordinarily used to cover the repair of underground cables. At least two direction finders were required to locate the general area in which a radio was broadcasting; each device would take a bearing, and where the lines crossed on the map would be the site of the station.

Success, however, was far from instant. To elude their pursuers, the transmitter operators changed frequencies and schedules and kept their broadcasts short so that the Germans would not have time to take bearings on the signals. It was late October, four months after the first transmissions were intercepted, before the teams got close to the three buildings in Berlin that housed the radios. Just then, a radio operator from the Red Orchestra

named Hans Coppi happened to notice the license plates on one of the equipment-carrying vehicles. It bore the telltale letters *WL*—for Wehrmacht/Luftwaffe. Coppi instantly alerted his piano-playing colleagues, and the Berlin Red Orchestra fell silent.

Attention now focused on the original transmitter, the one with the PTX call sign. The music emanating from this piano increased in volume—up to five hours every night—presumably in an attempt to make up for the silence from Berlin. Bearings taken by long-range direction finders narrowed the search to Belgium. The investigation there was assigned to the counterespionage branch of German military intelligence, Abwehr Section IIIF. Its chief was a forty-eight-year-old reserve captain named Harry Piepe. A veteran of World War I and a lawyer in peacetime, Piepe had been called back to serve as commander of an antitank company during the invasion of France. But the Abwehr learned of his long experience as a government magistrate—an official who approved the arrest of miscreants and then interrogated them—and posted him to Belgium as a member of Section IIIF.

In late November, the search centered on Brussels, and Berlin sent Piepe a radio-monitoring detachment equipped with the latest portable direction-finding gear. Carrying this unobtrusive equipment, which fit into a suitcase with a built-in aerial, Piepe and his surveillance team followed the music. At one point, the captain installed a direction finder in a little Fieseler Storch observation plane and took bearings while circling the city. In less than two weeks, Piepe and his men pinpointed a row house at 101 rue des Atrébates in the Etterbeek section of Brussels.

On the night of December 13, the captain and a platoon of thirty-five soldiers surrounded the three-story house and then burst in. Piepe ar-

On a Paris rooftop, German soldiers adjust the apparatus that helped track down hidden radio transmitters being used by agents of the Soviet spy network, the "Red Orchestra." The directional antenna was moved about the city until it picked up the same suspect signal from two different locations; the intersection of the two lines of direction marked the position of the clandestine transmitter.

rested two women and the radio operator, who was eventually identified as a Russian. The raiders confiscated the transmitter, which was still warm, and discovered in a fireplace a half-burnt document covered with ciphers. Behind a secret door, the Germans found a workshop containing blank passports and official forms and stamps. It was a "forger's paradise," Piepe recalled. "I simply couldn't believe it. This implied the existence of a really vast network, with tentacles everywhere."

The most tantalizing discovery in the forger's workshop were two photographs. One of the women identified the men as the leaders of the espionage ring, known to her only as *Le Grand Chef et Le Petit Chef*—"the Big Chief and the Little Chief." Piepe did not know it yet, but the Big Chief was Leopold Trepper, a Polish-born Communist who conducted the Red Orchestra; the Little Chief was Edward Kent, the alias of Victor Sukolov-Gurevich, a Russian-born espionage agent and Trepper's deputy. As Piepe studied the photographs, however, he had the "uncanny feeling" that he had seen the two men before.

He had, indeed. Although it took a while to dawn on him, the men were his next-door neighbors. To maintain his own cover as a Dutch merchant, Piepe had rented an office at 192 rue Royale. The office next door—beyond a "dividing wall so thin that we could hear one another," said Piepe—belonged to a company called Simexco. Ostensibly, Simexco was an international importer, procuring materials and machines for German occupation authorities; in reality, it provided both money and a cover for the Red Orchestra. Little Chief Kent headed Simexco; Big Chief Trepper was in charge of a sister firm in Paris called Simex that did extensive business with the Todt Organization, the Reich's immense military construction arm. "I'd passed them on the stairs a dozen times," Piepe later recalled. "We used to meet on the landing and tip our hats to one another."

As fate would have it, Trepper slipped through Piepe's fingers on the very day after the capture of the transmitter. Thinking nothing amiss, the Big Chief arrived at the house for a scheduled meeting with one of his operatives. That agent, dressed like a poor peasant with a basket full of live rabbits for sale, had been scooped up upon arrival. A few minutes later, Trepper knocked at the door. When a German soldier answered, the quick-thinking Chief produced an official-looking document stating that he, "Jean Gilbert" of Simex, had been authorized by the Todt Organization to search for strategic materials. Piepe was not present, but the soldier telephoned him about what to do with the new arrival. Captain Piepe curtly ordered the soldier to let this Jean Gilbert go about his business. "We were still amateurs," Piepe said later. "We still had to learn our trade."

Piepe learned fast—and he had an expert teacher. Early in 1942, he

joined forces with Karl Giering, a veteran Gestapo officer dispatched by Berlin to assist the investigation. Abwehr officers normally detested their rivals in the SS. But Giering was a magistrate's son with a long policeman's career dating back to pre-Nazi days, and Piepe found him congenial. He was in his early forties and hoarse-voiced from a cancer of the throat; he had a habit of drinking great quantities of the "cure" he insisted doctors had prescribed: coffee and brandy.

Over the next several months, the team of Piepe and Giering traced, then shadowed the forger, Abraham Raichman, whose well-equipped workshop had been found at 101 rue des Atrébates. On Gestapo orders, a collaborating Belgian police inspector contacted Raichman and won his friendship by professing sympathy for the Soviet cause. Raichman was so taken in that he even hid his radio transmitter in the inspector's garage. The forger then unwittingly led Piepe to a rendezvous with Konstantin Yefremov, the Russian army captain who had replaced Kent (who had gone into hiding after the rue des Atrébates raid) as head of the Red Orchestra in Belgium. In due course, Yefremov was hauled in and induced to cooperate with the spy catchers. His information later led to the capture in Amsterdam of a major agent: the chief of the Orchestra's entire Dutch section.

The day Piepe nabbed Yefremov—July 30, 1942—was a very good one for the German agents. That evening, Piepe led a night raid on the house harboring the Orchestra's last piano in Brussels. The transmissions had been traced by Piepe's old friends, the direction finders, who by now were so expert that they could virtually point out which room housed a transmitter. The radio experts concluded that the clandestine set must be hidden in the attic—and sure enough, the searchers found it there, humming away, with the window open. "The man who had been working here was jumping from chimney to chimney firing shots to drive us off," recalled Piepe. When Piepe's men finally caught up with him hiding in a nearby cellar under an overturned bathtub, he turned out to be quite

a prize: Johann Wenzel, an old-line German Communist long sought by the Gestapo and such an accomplished spy that he was dubbed the Professor.

Meanwhile, cryptanalysts in Berlin had been laboring to divine the identities of other players in the Red Orchestra. Signals Security had assembled a team of a dozen or so specialists in mathematics and linguistics

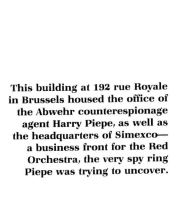

Abwehr Captain Harry Piepe *(top)* assumed a new identity when he began tracking a ring of Soviet agents in western Europe. As a jovial Dutch merchant named Riepert *(bottom)*, he led the hunt for a clandestine radio operating in Brussels.

This building at 192 rue Royale in Brussels housed the office of the Abwehr counterespionage agent Harry Piepe, as well as the headquarters of Simexco—a business front for the Red Orchestra, the very spy ring Piepe was trying to uncover.

under Wilhelm Vauck, a schoolmaster and reserve army lieutenant. Vauck concentrated on the charred document that Piepe's men had salvaged from the fireplace of 101 rue des Atrébates. With its columns of numbers, it appeared to be a grid from which messages were encoded. In six weeks of exhaustive work, Vauck and his team managed to reconstruct a single word from the grid. The word was *proctor*.

Since the Russians were known to base their codes on sentences in obscure works of fiction, the discovery launched an intensive literary search. One of the women arrested at the house recalled the titles of five novels kept on a desk there. The counterintelligence agents scoured bookstores and found four of the novels. But the word *proctor* did not appear in any of them, and the investigators could not turn up a copy of the fifth volume until mid-May, when an agent came across it in a secondhand bookshop in Paris. In the book appeared a character named Proctor.

Vauck's code breakers then tackled some 300 messages intercepted from the Moscow-Brussels traffic. Nearly one-third contained a clue that led to a sentence from the Proctor book. With the key sentences in hand, the cryptanalysts could now decode the messages. Information about such matters as arms production and unit strengths fell from the decoded ciphers, but there were no revelations as to the membership of the Red Orchestra.

Then, in July, the code breakers' perseverance paid off. They deciphered a message sent the previous October from Moscow to Edward Kent, the Little Chief, who was then in Brussels. At that time the Orchestra's transmitters in Berlin had shut down to elude German direction-finding sleuths, and Moscow wanted Kent to travel to Berlin to investigate. To the amazement of the Germans reading the order, Moscow had listed the addresses of the Orchestra's three leaders in Berlin.

Within forty-eight hours, the Gestapo had identified the trio and had them under close surveillance. All were prominent Germans. One was an author, another a senior official in the Reich Economics Ministry,

Luftwaffe officer Harro Schulze-Boysen and his wife, Libertas, shown here after their 1936 wedding, served the Kremlin well as Soviet agents in Berlin. The couple's connections in Berlin society yielded much information to pass on to Moscow.

and the third a socially prominent Luftwaffe lieutenant. The most sensitively placed was the lieutenant, Harro Schulze-Boysen, a thirty-two-year-old intelligence specialist with access to much secret material at Luftwaffe headquarters. A grandnephew of the revered Grand Admiral Alfred von Tirpitz, Schulze-Boysen turned out to be such a recklessly romantic Communist idealist that it was a wonder no one had caught on to him before. Among other things, he was given to such stunts as stalking the streets at night in full uniform to paste up anti-Nazi posters.

Schulze-Boysen and his colleagues had recruited their network by means of various inducements ranging from sexual favors to an appeal to anti-Nazi German patriotism. Colonel Joachim Rohleder, chief of Abwehr counterespionage, later characterized the enemy agents as "bloody amateurs." But the Orchestra nevertheless got its hands on some highly

To the Marseilles street photographer who took their picture in 1942, Edward Kent and Margarete Barcza were just another strolling couple. In reality, Kent was actually Victor Sukolov-Gurevich, the fugitive second-in-command of the Red Orchestra. Barcza, his mistress, was unaware of his espionage work.

important information. Over the past fourteen months, Schulze-Boysen and his colleagues had sent Moscow more than 500 messages that not only described new weapons and other military secrets but also detailed the developing tensions between Hitler and his generals.

One recruit, Corporal Horst Heilmann, who seemed to have been among the many lovers of Schulze-Boysen's wife, worked in the code-breaking section of Signals Security—right under the nose of Wilhelm Vauck himself. But the low-ranking Heilmann did not learn that Schulze-Boysen and the others had been discovered until August 29, when a colleague showed him the incriminating message from Moscow. Heilmann telephoned Schulze-Boysen's apartment to warn him but had to leave word with the maid. When Schulze-Boysen returned the call that night, Heilmann had left the office, and Vauck, who was working late, answered his phone. The spy asked to leave a message and gave his name. Vauck, dumbfounded on hearing it, asked lamely, "Do you spell your name with a 'Y'?" The caller said that he did.

That bizarre twist forced the Gestapo's hand. By shadowing the Orchestra leaders, tapping their phones, and opening their mail, the spy catchers had hoped to build up a clear picture of the ring and then roll it up all at once. Now, fearing that their investigation had been exposed, they decided to strike before Schulze-Boysen could alert the others. On the morning of August 30, the black cars began making their rounds. They soon returned with Schulze-Boysen, his wife, and the other leaders.

At first the prisoners presented a solid front. But the Gestapo brought in its top interrogators with instructions to spare no effort. That did not necessarily imply wholesale torture, for despite the Gestapo's fearsome reputation, physical intimidation of spies was by regulation closely supervised. According to Gestapo rules, "intensified interrogation"—Himmler's euphemism for torture—could be employed only after application

in writing to the chief of the Security Police, and even then only in the presence of an SS doctor.

Other techniques worked as well, or better. Gestapo agents masquerading as prisoners shared the cells of Orchestra members. Schulze-Boysen's wife, Libertas, broke silence after a Gestapo typist pretended to befriend her. Other tongues loosened, and by mid-October, a total of 116 Orchestra suspects were in jail. But few Germans would learn of it until after the war. Hitler was acutely embarrassed by such betrayal by the German elite in the very heart of the Reich, and he decreed that the crushing of the Red Orchestra must proceed in utmost secrecy.

While the Gestapo mopped up in Berlin, Piepe and Giering and a twenty-man task force moved to Paris. Although the Belgian, Dutch, and German branches of the Red Orchestra had been broken, the Big Chief and the Little Chief were still at large, and all the clues as to their whereabouts pointed to France: Surveillance of Simexco headquarters in Brussels had revealed heavy phone and mail traffic with Simex in Paris.

Piepe and Giering began closing in. An official of the Todt Organization, with which Simex did the greater part of its business, identified the photograph of Leopold Trepper found in the Brussels house as that of Jean Gilbert, the company's managing director. The Germans began laying traps to snare the elusive Trepper. But Trepper "had a good nose," Piepe recalled, and slipped away.

Meanwhile, the counterintelligence team had better luck with the Little Chief. The forger from Brussels, Abraham Raichman, helped lead the Germans to Edward Kent,

An air of prosperity helped Leopold Trepper win the confidence—and the business—of German authorities. Trepper, Moscow's top spy in western Europe, ran a firm in Paris whose main client was the Todt Organization, the Reich's huge military construction arm.

who was arrested in Marseilles on November 12. Kent was returned to Brussels, and while Giering was there questioning him, one of his Gestapo deputies nearly blew the continuing search for the Big Chief. Without informing Giering, the deputy staged a premature raid on Simex headquarters on the Champs Élysées. Trepper responded by making plans for the ultimate sham: He would stage his own death in a rural town, with a

funeral and a death certificate. But before fleeing Paris, he had one important appointment to keep—with his dentist, to have two teeth capped, at 2:00 p.m. on November 24.

On the morning of the 24th, Giering was grilling the wife of one of Trepper's agents arrested in the raid at Simex. Terrified, the woman desperately racked her brain for some clue that would help the Germans find the Big Chief and persuade them to go easy on her husband. Suddenly she remembered that "Monsieur Gilbert" had complained of a toothache and that her husband had recommended the family dentist. The Big Chief was in the dentist's chair that afternoon when Giering and Piepe burst in, guns drawn, trembling with excitement. "Bravo!" Trepper said coolly as Giering clamped on the handcuffs. "You've done your work well."

The capture of Trepper was the crowning triumph of German counterintelligence up to that point in the war, and he was treated with great care in expectation of the information he might reveal. Giering sat day after day with him, drinking cognac and coffee, trading spy stories, and gently prying loose the names of his lieutenants. Early in 1943, Giering and Piepe could report to Berlin the roundup of the last remnants of the Red Orchestra.

And now, with the cooperation of Trepper and some of his pianists, the Orchestra played on under its new German conductors. Hoping to emulate the success of the Abwehr's Operation North Pole, Himmler's RSHA launched its own playback game with Moscow. Using captured transmitters, the Germans responded to Moscow's commands for information with such tidbits as the makeup of certain German army units in western Europe. Moscow, in turn, was sufficiently indiscreet for the RSHA to unearth a number of other Communist networks in France.

The radio games began to fade, however, only a few months after the debut of this phony Red Orchestra. Trepper's chief pianist, Johann Wenzel, escaped, and the Brussels transmitter had to be shut down. Moreover, German army commanders in western Europe refused to supply RSHA with the increasingly sensitive intelligence demanded by Moscow. Then, on September 13, 1943, ten months after his capture, the Big Chief took leave of his Gestapo hosts. While visiting a Paris pharmacy, he managed to trick his escort and escape, bringing down the baton on the Orchestra.

After the war, Trepper insisted that he had only pretended to collaborate with the Germans. It was merely a ruse, he said, to gain German trust and divert the enemy from other agents. True or not, the story did not prevent Trepper's Soviet masters from sending him to prison for ten years. Still, it was a better fate than befell many of his former colleagues in the Orchestra. Like others caught in the web of counterespionage, they paid for their intrigues at the hands of Nazi executioners. ✚

The Enigma of German Ciphers

By the time the war broke out, German cryptanalysts and their Allied counterparts had long been adversaries in a clandestine struggle for supremacy in the world of secret communications. Early in the contest, Germany held the upper hand. Prewar Germany possessed the securest military communications in the world, thanks to an ingenious device called Enigma—a cipher machine so sophisticated that its users believed it to be impregnable. But German confidence in Enigma was misplaced: First in Poland, then in France and England, dedicated teams of code breakers attacked the cipher in utmost secrecy and with increasing success. Their work would change the course of the war.

Enigma originated in 1923 as a commercial cipher machine used by firms that wanted to protect their communications from exposure to competitors. The device, which resembled a typewriter, encoded messages one letter at a time for later transmission by telegraph or radio. Each time an operator pressed one of the twenty-six keys, an electrical impulse coursed through a maze of circuitry, finally lighting a bulb that illuminated the enciphered letter on an alphabet panel. The pressure on the key also caused a mechanical rotor to turn, altering the electrical pathway that the next pulse would take; millions of different encoding combinations were possible.

In the late 1920s, the German military adapted the commercial machine for its own use, adding features such as a

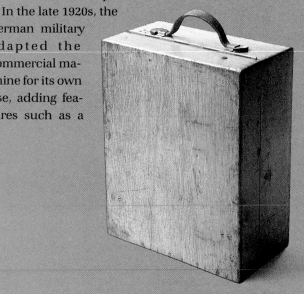

plugboard that brought a new layer of complexity to Enigma ciphers. Nonetheless, within a few years Polish intelligence was routinely reading Enigma traffic, by virtue of meticulous analysis combined with several strokes of luck. Throughout the 1930s, the Poles managed to stay abreast of improvements to Enigma machines, and they passed their expertise on to the British. The struggle to decipher Enigma continued throughout the war; periods of amazing success alternated with dismal failure as the Germans added new features or changed operating techniques. Twice, then a third time, the Allies cracked increasingly complex versions of the Enigma naval code, helping British and American ships to defend against the U-boat fleet and ultimately defeat Germany in the Battle of the Atlantic.

Enigma intercepts also played a major role in the North African theater. In 1942, at the gates of Egypt, General Erwin Rommel experienced critical shortages of equipment and fuel. When Berlin radioed details about supply convoys coming to Rommel's relief, British and American listeners were able to dispatch warships, submarines, and aircraft to intercept the German vessels, with devastating effect. At the front, when Rommel prepared for a do-or-die breakthrough to Cairo in August 1942, the British Eighth Army learned of his plans through Enigma decoders and was ready when Rommel launched his attack. The German forces were dealt a stunning blow from which they never recovered. Rommel realized that his plan must have been betrayed but had no idea how.

The Germans' faith in Enigma remained unshaken throughout the war: 200,000 machines were issued by war's end, to the great benefit of Germany's foes.

Besides the customary three rotors, this military Enigma machine has a plugboard in the front, which increased its encoding combinations. Weighing twenty-six pounds and measuring 7 x 11 x 13 inches when packed up (left), the battery-powered device was portable and completely self-contained, operable in a ship, an airplane, a truck, or at corps headquarters.

A Labyrinth for Electrical Pulses

To decode an Enigma message, the circuitry of the receiver's machine had to be set identically to that of the sender's. The receiver had to know which rotors to insert, in what order to insert them, and how to position each one. German military commands issued manuals to their Enigma operators listing the circuitry settings, which changed regularly. The receiver of an Enigma message simply punched in the cipher letters, and the machine, operating in reverse, produced the letters of the plaintext.

This Enigma has three rotors *(top)*, a lamp board, a keyboard, and a plugboard.

A web of wires within an Enigma rotor links flat contact points on one side with spring-loaded brushes on the other.

Each change of circuitry required the Enigma operator to rearrange the rotors on their axle and change the setting of each rotor by twisting its lettered or numbered ring into a new position while holding the toothed sprocket stationary.

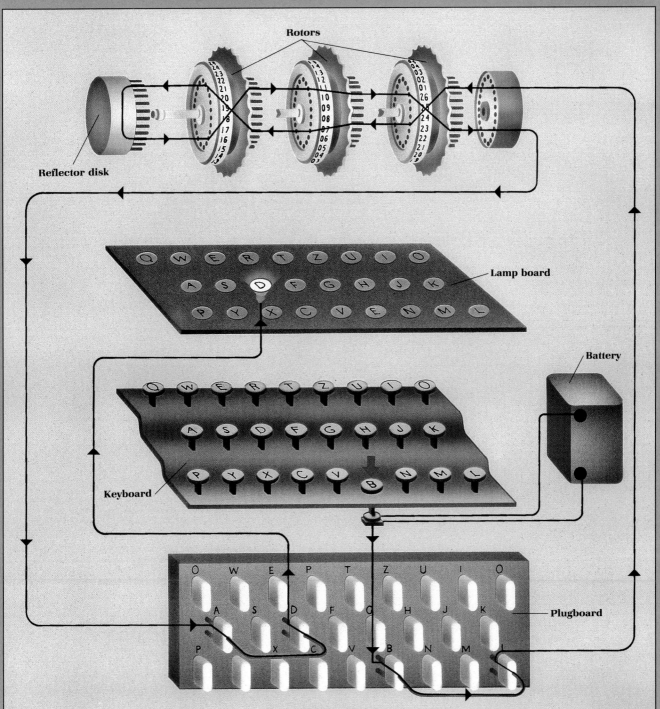

Rotors

Reflector disk

Lamp board

Battery

Keyboard

Plugboard

Pressing a key on the Enigma keyboard (here, the letter *B*) starts an electrical impulse on a complex path through the machine. Powered by a battery *(right)*, the pulse undergoes its first substitution at the plugboard, where a cable transposes it from the *B* socket to the *L* socket. Reaching the rotor section *(top)*, the pulse moves through the *L* contact on a

stationary ring into the spring-loaded brush on the first rotor. Transposed again by the rotor wiring, it emerges as a different letter on the other side; each successive rotor repeats this process. Turned around and changed yet again by the wiring of a reflector disk, the electricity follows another circuitous route back through the three rotors and the plugboard before

reaching the lamp board, where the encrypted letter, a *D*, glows. When the key is pressed, the first rotor advances one position, changing the electrical pathway for the next plaintext letter. When the first rotor completes one full revolution (after twenty-six letters), the second rotor moves ahead one position; the third rotor advances when the second completes a revolution.

An Enigma unit serves General Heinz Guderian (*standing*) **directing the blitzkrieg in France from his command vehicle.**

Keeping Secrets in the Field

Enigma proved its worth to the Wehrmacht during the blitzkrieg that overran Poland in 1939 and France in 1940. The fast-moving units of the army, particularly the panzers, relied on radio during these campaigns to maintain contact with one another and with headquarters. Commanders needed to issue orders in a timely but secure manner, and headquarters at all levels required regular reports detailing the location and strength of each unit and the disposition of the enemy troops they faced. Battery-powered Enigma machines, which could go anywhere a field radio went, met all of the Army's tactical requirements.

Operators usually worked in teams of two, with one person pushing the keys and the other recording the encoded letter that glowed on the lamp board. Even so, the pace was slow; although the Enigma looked like a typewriter, pressing its keys required sufficient force to advance the rotors. The enciphered text was passed to a radio operator, who used Morse code to send it to its destination. The receiver punched in the coded letters, and the plaintext equivalents appeared on the lamp board.

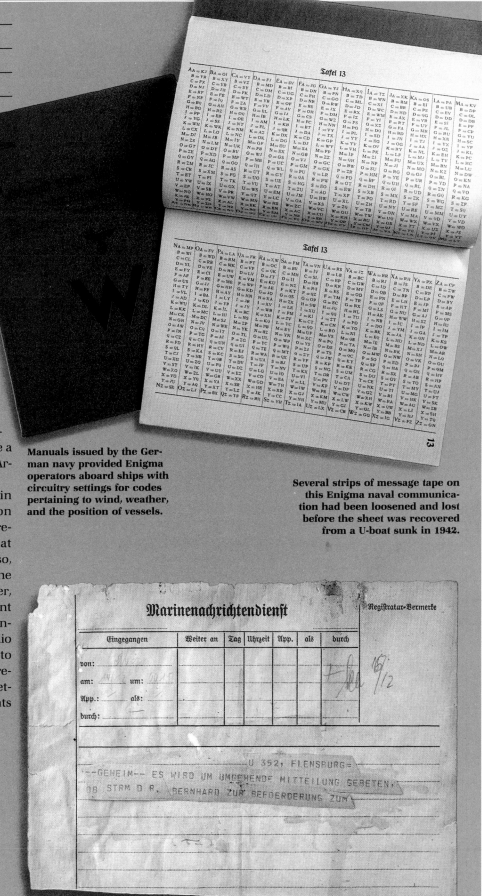

Manuals issued by the German navy provided Enigma operators aboard ships with circuitry settings for codes pertaining to wind, weather, and the position of vessels.

Several strips of message tape on this Enigma naval communication had been loosened and lost before the sheet was recovered from a U-boat sunk in 1942.

Cryptanalysts Henryk Zygalski
(left), Jerzy Rozycki, and Marian
Rejewski, who unraveled the
mysteries of Enigma, stroll
together in France after fleeing
Poland ahead of the German
invasion. Rejewski and Zygalski
reached England via Spain
in 1942; Rozycki went down
with a ship the same year.

Unraveling the Mystery of a Machine

Wary of Germany's aggressive intentions, Poland mounted a painstaking effort to crack the Enigma cipher and eavesdrop on its neighbor during the 1930s. This endeavor received a boost in 1929 when, unknown to its German owners, a military Enigma fell briefly into Polish hands, and cryptanalysts were able to examine it and make diagrams of its circuitry.

Polish mathematicians went on to devise ingenious analytical machines, including replica Enigmas and a "bombe" (so called because it ticked as it worked) to sift through the enormous number of possible plug and rotor combinations.

Poland's ally France shared important discoveries, including a code book and sample encryptions obtained through a German traitor. In 1939, with war imminent, the Poles passed along all their cryptographical information to the French and the British, giving one Enigma replica to England and another to France; two more later made their way to France with fleeing cryptanalysts.

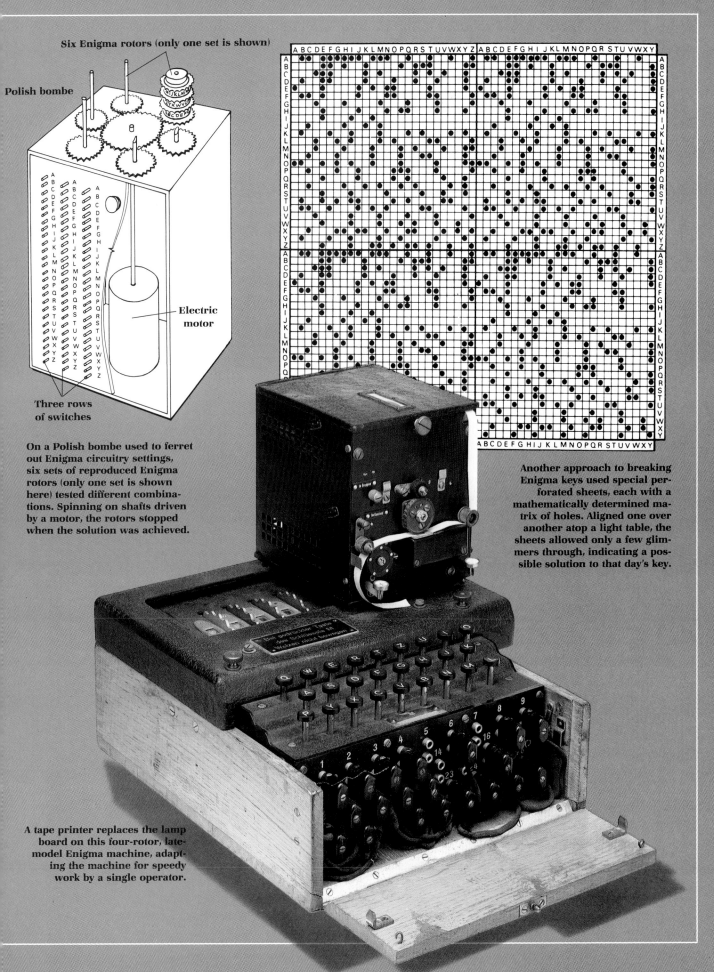

Six Enigma rotors (only one set is shown)

Polish bombe

Electric
motor

Three rows
of switches

On a Polish bombe used to ferret out Enigma circuitry settings, six sets of reproduced Enigma rotors (only one set is shown here) tested different combinations. Spinning on shafts driven by a motor, the rotors stopped when the solution was achieved.

Another approach to breaking Enigma keys used special perforated sheets, each with a mathematically determined matrix of holes. Aligned one over another atop a light table, the sheets allowed only a few glimmers through, indicating a possible solution to that day's key.

A tape printer replaces the lamp board on this four-rotor, late-model Enigma machine, adapting the machine for speedy work by a single operator.

Bletchley Park mansion was headquarters to numerous cryptographic units like this Royal Air Force contingent *(inset)*.

The Powers of Ultra

British intelligence took up the Enigma challenge with the same urgency as the Poles. Scores of cryptanalysts, mathematicians, and engineers were recruited to work at Bletchley Park, a sprawling country estate fifty miles from London. After 1941, they were joined by a number of Americans. Most who worked at the tightly guarded intelligence complex remained for the duration; they knew too many secrets to be transferred.

The work of breaking Enigma keys was repeated daily; some, including the important Luftwaffe cipher, routinely yielded after a few hours. With the key in hand, the Bletchley experts were able to decipher the rest of the day's messages. Teams of translators and analysts pored over the messages, gleaning nuggets of information that were sent to high-level operational commanders. Designated *Ultra*, this information sometimes reached Allied forces just a few hours after the original message was sent.

Replica Enigma rotors crowd the face of a British bombe; far more powerful than the earlier Polish version, the code-cracking machine stood six feet high.

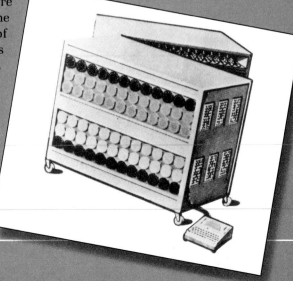

A United States Navy Wave adjusts settings on a bombe in Washington, D.C., where hundreds of Waves ran the secret machines.

FOUR

The Audacious Irregulars

The skies over Italy were studded with clouds as a small fleet of Luftwaffe tow planes and gliders bore north from Rome toward the Apennines. The ninety paratroopers who were crowded into the eight flimsy gliders were uncomfortable and uneasy; all they could see were the flickers of changing light through the thick, opaque cellophane of their side windows.

In the lead glider on that afternoon of September 12, 1943, a huge man dressed in the uniform of a Waffen-SS captain twisted restlessly in his seat. Finally, unwilling to trust the navigator, he pulled out a knife and slashed a hole in his craft's canvas skin. Peering out of his crude peephole through gaps in the clouds, he glimpsed the bridges, roads, and river bends familiar to him from maps. After some minutes, he recognized his destination—the snowbound Gran Sasso d'Italia, high in the Apennines.

"Helmets on," commanded the captain, as a ski lodge perched on the rocky mountain crest came into view. "Slip the towropes!" One after another the gliders were cut loose, and the rush of wind replaced the roar of engines as the tow planes flew off. The glider pilots banked in a wide circle to descend toward the triangular meadow where they were to land. But as they approached, they received a nasty surprise.

The SS captain had seen the area only a few days before, photographing it from a bucking Heinkel 111 reconnaissance plane flying at 15,000 feet in turbulent winds. The meadow that appeared flat then, now presented a dismayingly different profile. "It was triangular, all right," recalled the captain. "But far from being flat, it was a steep, a very steep hillside. It could even have been a ski jump."

Common sense—and express orders from his superior—dictated that the captain abort his mission and order the gliders down to the relative safety of the valley. But Otto Skorzeny chose a monumental gamble. He yelled an order to crash-land, and his pilot dove for the hill.

With a shriek of metal and a ripping of canvas, the fragile craft slammed into the hillside and slid to a stop not sixteen yards from the lodge. Out tumbled its passengers, miraculously unhurt. The other seven gliders came hurtling down behind. One disintegrated when a sudden gust of wind

As the head of a special forces unit during the war, SS Lieut. Colonel Otto Skorzeny displayed the same boldness that earned him dueling scars during his student days in Vienna. "You cannot waste time on feinting and sidestepping," he wrote of his tactics. "You must decide on your target and go in."

In September 1943, the pilot of a Fieseler Storch reconnaissance plane with Otto Skorzeny and Benito Mussolini on board prepares to take off from Gran Sasso, in Italy's Apennine range. Skorzeny and his men rescued the Italian dictator from anti-Fascists holding him at a ski lodge on the mountain.

drove it into a jagged outcrop; all ten men aboard were severely injured. But the others delivered their cargoes of German troops more or less intact.

Skorzeny, his men running behind him, dashed up the slope past a handful of startled Italian guards and entered the first door he came to. It was a radio room; pausing only to smash the set with the butt of his machine pistol, the burly SS man retraced his steps, scaled a ten-foot wall, and charged the main hotel entrance. Looking up, he spied a well-known face at a window. He raced down a corridor, up a flight of stairs, and burst into the room. Standing before him in the custody of two Italian officers was a stocky, unshaven man dressed in ill-fitting civilian clothes. Skorzeny drew himself up to his full six feet four and addressed the tired-looking figure. "Duce!" he announced. "The Führer has sent me! You are free!"

To Italian dictator Benito Mussolini, who until that moment had been seriously contemplating suicide, the sight of this strapping SS officer and his swarm of commandos must have seemed like something out of a giddy dream. Two months earlier, Italy's Fascist state had collapsed like a house of cards in the wake of the Allied invasion of Sicily. On July 25, the duce had been ejected from power and placed under arrest in a lightning coup that even his heavily armed bodyguard division had not opposed. It was clear that Italy, war-weary and demoralized, was finished as an Axis ally. Acknowledging the inevitable, the German high command had recommended a withdrawal to the north, leaving Mussolini to his fate.

But Adolf Hitler had been outraged at the mere suggestion. Any thought

of retreating from Italy was defeatist, he screamed. Never would he abandon his friend Mussolini, and he ordered Himmler to prepare an immediate plan to rescue the duce and return him to power in Italy.

The operation had been entrusted to Skorzeny, nicknamed Scarface for a dueling scar that ran across his left cheek from ear to chin. Only a few months earlier, Skorzeny had been chosen to lead a new SS unit charged with special operations in foreign and neutral countries. The Mussolini rescue was the thirty-five-year-old captain's first mission in his new command and his first opportunity to display a remarkable flair for derring-do.

Within minutes of his startling appearance on Gran Sasso, Skorzeny had accepted the surrender of the Italian troops guarding the hotel. He swiftly put a detail to work clearing boulders from the meadow to create a crude airstrip. Meanwhile, SS and Luftwaffe reinforcements, accompanied by a photographer to record the stirring events, arrived via funicular railway from the valley below. A Fieseler Storch liaison plane circled overhead.

The plane touched down as soon as a strip had been cleared, and Mussolini was bundled aboard. Brusquely overruling the pilot's furious insistence that the plane would crash under the added weight, Skorzeny himself then clambered in and squeezed his bulky frame behind the dictator. The tiny aircraft leaped forward, bounced precariously across the meadow, careened over the edge of the precipice, and disappeared from view. For a few sickening seconds, it plummeted toward the valley floor; then the pilot wrestled it under control and flew at top speed to Rome. There Mussolini and his rescuer transferred to a waiting Heinkel and winged north into the Reich. By midnight, the two men were exchanging ribald jokes in a comfortable suite in Vienna's Hotel Imperial.

Adolf Hitler was ecstatic. Before the night was out he had promoted Skorzeny to major, had awarded him the Knight's Cross of the Iron Cross, and had telephoned with congratulations. "You have performed a military feat that will become part of history," declared the Führer emotionally. Two days later, Skorzeny was at the Wolf's Lair in East Prussia, enjoying a late-night tête-à-tête with Hitler. The following day, he lunched with Bormann and Himmler, took a stroll with Göring, and had tea with Ribbentrop as the Nazi hierarchy made speed to honor the Reich's newest hero.

In truth, Skorzeny's feat was of little practical value. Installed as puppet ruler of German-occupied northern Italy, the feckless Mussolini was despised by his countrymen and powerless to bring about the Fascist revival Hitler had envisioned. The Gran Sasso rescue was a bonanza nonetheless. The Third Reich in the autumn of 1943 was reeling from a series of devastating military defeats and in desperate need of something to cheer about. Propaganda Minister Goebbels paraded Skorzeny before adoring

crowds and blanketed the nation with newspaper, magazine, and radio accounts of the mission; a film crew traveled to Gran Sasso to reenact the heroic deed for moviegoers.

Even the Allies were impressed. Winston Churchill gave a full account of the mission in a speech before the House of Commons. "The stroke was one of great daring," rumbled the British prime minister. "It certainly shows there are many possibilities of this kind open in modern warfare."

Churchill's praise for Skorzeny's mission reflected his own enthusiasm for such operations. The Gran Sasso raid was a particularly sensational and well publicized example of a type of warfare normally cloaked in secrecy. In this shadowy cousin of conventional combat, elite, highly trained units slipped behind enemy lines to carry out all manner of missions, from sabotage and subversion to seizing strategic targets in advance of regular troops. Kidnapping and assassination would be in a day's work—as would the wearing of enemy uniforms if necessary for disguise.

Although rooted in a tradition of wartime deception as old as the Trojan Horse, special forces were nevertheless generally regarded with distaste by regular soldiers, who saw in their clandestine, anonymous activities the skills of the warrior corrupted by the work of the spy and murderer. And yet neither side in the Second World War shrank from taking advantage of such talents. Britain had its famed Commandos, the United States its Rangers—and Germany entered the war with its Brandenburgers, crack troops raised and trained by intelligence chief Wilhelm Canaris's Abwehr. With its great diversity of skills and languages, the Brandenburg unit was one of the Abwehr's proudest possessions—and a much-coveted prize in the continuing internecine struggle with the SS for absolute control of the Reich's security and intelligence apparatus.

As the war progressed and the Reich's fortunes declined, the lightly armed Brandenburgers would be misused as regular infantry and hurled into the mincing machine of the Russian front, from which they would never recover. Meanwhile, the SS would form its own special forces, in which Otto Skorzeny would loom even larger than life, and which would gradually preempt the role of the increasingly demoralized and ineffective Abwehr units. In time, virtually all intelligence activities would fall to the SS. And the renowned Canaris—isolated, charged with an ever-growing catalog of Abwehr failures, a suspected traitor for his anti-Nazi sentiments, himself sick at heart over his country's course—would be arrested and sent to prison until the time came for his execution.

It is remarkable that any sort of special forces unit ever was born into the German army, considering the visceral repugnance of its leaders for irregular troops. Imbued with an almost mystical reverence for their calling, the German officers' corps virtually to a man regarded special operations as not only perfidious but as a direct slur on their personal honor and that of their nation; to creep in an enemy's uniform was to sully one's own. Largely as a result of this attitude, the German army had failed, as a rule, to produce men adept at unconventional operations.

One of the few exceptions was General Paul von Lettow-Vorbeck, the World War I commander of a small colonial force in German East Africa. Vastly outnumbered by his Allied foes, Lettow-Vorbeck had successfully employed guerrilla tactics to tie up large numbers of British troops that might otherwise have fought in Europe. That lesson made a lasting impression on one of his junior officers, Captain Theodor von Hippel, who after the war was assigned to the Abwehr's Section II, the branch of military intelligence responsible for clandestine operations.

As well as being inspired by his old commander, Hippel was fascinated by the wartime exploits—considerably exaggerated in the telling—of T. E. Lawrence, the British adventurer known to the world as Lawrence of Arabia. Lawrence was one of a group of British agents who encouraged Arab tribesmen to harass Turkish forces in the Middle East, and Hippel was convinced that similar guerrilla techniques could be applied to regular German military operations. His idea was for small, elite formations to open the door for regular forces. By infiltrating enemy lines before an offensive—even before war was declared—these units could secure bridges, road junctions, and key communications facilities; they could disseminate false intelligence, blow up supply dumps, attack enemy headquarters, and generally sow chaos out of all proportion to their numbers.

The imaginative Hippel suggested that the natural home for such an organization would be within Admiral Canaris's covert Section II. The suggestion flew in the face of Wehrmacht sensibilities. But German military thinking was evolving rapidly, and Hippel's idea was not far removed from one of the most innovative of the new concepts, that of armored blitzkrieg warfare. The central idea behind blitzkrieg was the reliance on lightning speed and mobility to counter enemy superiority—a tactic that dovetailed with the kind of clandestine shock attacks that Hippel had in mind.

Sometime in late 1938 or early 1939—evidently at the request of the High Command of the Armed Forces—Section II began interviewing volunteers for a special provisional unit under Hippel. Men were recruited in strictest secrecy, and their early activities remain a mystery; but they clearly were intended for use in the invasion of Poland, when blitzkrieg would be unveiled in all its overwhelming fury. By the summer of 1939, the Abwehr had trained several groups of Polish-speaking volunteers and incorporated

Admiral Wilhelm Canaris *(center)*
inspects the Brandenburgers at
their camp west of Berlin. To the
admiral's left is Captain Theodor
von Hippel, founder of the unit.

them into a battalion-size unit called the Ebbinghaus Battle Group.

A few days before the invasion, small parties of these men, disguised as coal miners and workers, began slipping into Poland and infiltrating the mines, factory complexes, and electric power stations of Silesia, the center of Poland's heavy industry. Other members of Hippel's command crossed the frontier on the night of August 31 and positioned themselves at several bridges across the Vistula River, a major artery down the center of the country. By the time the Wehrmacht came roaring into Poland on the morning of September 1, the Ebbinghaus group had secured the tactically vital Vistula bridges and had captured intact a number of important Silesian industrial installations.

Official German accounts of the Polish blitz made no mention of the Abwehr's special units. Indeed, recommendations for the award of Iron Crosses were rejected because a state of war did not actually exist between Germany and Poland when the men first went into action. Despite the lack of recognition, however, Hippel's troops had proved their value beyond doubt, and Canaris decided to incorporate them formally into the Abwehr. On October 15, 1939, the first of these groups, the euphemistically designated Lehr und Bau Kompagnie z.b.V. 800, or Special Duty Training and Construction Company no. 800, was established. Its headquarters was in the old Prussian city of Brandenburg, giving the organization the name it would carry henceforth. Although under Abwehr control and thus outside the standard chain of command, the Brandenburgers were not professional spies or saboteurs but uniformed members of the armed forces recruited for special skills and trained for special duties. Their objectives were decided by the high command, and they were assigned as needed to individual army groups for specific missions.

One of the principal requirements for membership in a Brandenburg detachment was fluency in at least one foreign language, and the polyglot background of the recruits was an ominous herald of Hitler's ambition. There was no country in Europe in which at least one Brandenburger was not totally at home. Recruits were found among the *Volksdeutsche*, ethnic Germans who had lived outside the Reich's borders in eastern Europe and who spoke Czech, Polish, Ukrainian, or Ruthenian as well as the local dialects peculiar to those regions. There were Baltic Germans fluent in Estonian, Latvian, Lithuanian, Finnish—and, of course, Russian. Other Brandenburgers came from families that had colonized former German possessions in Africa or South America and were proficient in the native dialects of those areas, as well as in English, Portuguese, and Spanish. A number of Brandenburgers had command of six languages and a few of them could even handle such obscure tongues as Tibetan or Afghani.

In addition to their language skills, the men brought with them a treasure-trove of up-to-date passports, ration books, and identity papers that could be used to fabricate false documents for agents. And their familiarity with local habits and customs made them all but indistinguishable from natives and therefore able to blend effortlessly into an enemy population. A Brandenburger going into Russia, for example, would, in the words of one Abwehr agent, "know how to spit like a Russian."

On a large country estate outside Brandenburg, the future raiders were taught the techniques of stealth and self-sufficiency: how to move silently through forests, live off the land, navigate by the stars, and survive in the severest weather. They learned to handle kayaks, parachutes, and cross-country skis, and to produce explosives from such basic commodities as potash, flour, and confectioners' sugar. They became expert in the use of small arms—as well as the knife and the garrote. More than a few volunteers dropped out or were dismissed as the course proceeded; those who survived regarded themselves as the elite, as good as, or better than, any troops in the world.

The first test came on April 9, 1940, when a Danish-speaking Brandenburg platoon dressed in Danish uniform captured a vital bridge across the Little Belt Strait, easing the way for German forces in the invasion of Norway. A month later, Brandenburg units attached to the Sixth Army helped pave the way for the attacks on Belgium, Holland, and Luxembourg that opened the western campaign.

At two o'clock on the morning of May 10, Lieutenant Wilhelm Walther and eight other Brandenburgers, disguised as three Dutch military policemen escorting six disarmed German soldiers, crossed the frontier into the still-neutral Netherlands and walked three miles to the town of Gennep. There stood their objective: a railway bridge across the Meuse River into western Holland. In anticipation of a possible German attack, the Dutch had already wired the bridge with demolition charges, and a detail was poised to trigger the explosives at the first sign of a German troop train. But the sight of Walther's tiny party aroused no suspicions. The three Brandenburgers dressed as military policemen walked straight up to the guardhouse on the eastern bank and quickly overpowered the sentries. Their "prisoners" meanwhile swarmed over the bridge, quickly cutting the leads to the explosives. A few minutes later, the first armored train, followed by infantry-bearing freights, roared over the bridge, racing unimpeded into Holland to cover the northern flank of the German advance through Belgium and France.

Similar scenes were played out all along the 200-mile front that day. The Abwehr men were not universally successful, however. At Nijmegen on the

Meuse, the 100th Special Missions Infantry Battalion was beaten back with severe losses by Dutch troops who then blew two important bridges sky-high; and the assault on the bridge across the Rhine at Arnhem was a failure as well. Yet overall, wrote one Abwehr officer, "forty-two out of sixty-one objectives were secured and handed over to the units following behind." And this time, there was no ignoring the Brandenburgers' contribution: Iron Crosses were awarded to three-quarters of the 600 men involved. Their commander in chief, Adolf Hitler, was so well pleased that he ordered the Lehr un Bau Kompagnie z.b.V. 800 to be expanded to regimental size.

Some members of the German high command still regarded Canaris's troops as renegades. But many officers, noting the spectacular successes of the special forces in Belgium and Holland, declared themselves won over. Thereafter, the Abwehr units were in great demand and played a significant role in the continuing series of lightning German advances that marked the first years of the war. Whenever a major German assault went in, it was preceded by Abwehr special units carrying out such operations as seizing bridges over the Danube in the April 1941 takeover of Yugoslavia and then heading into the Soviet Union that June in advance of Operation Barbarossa, the mightiest invasion ever launched in the annals of war.

The Brandenburg Regiment was in the thick of the action throughout the triumphant opening months of the Russian campaign. Abwehr units seized the ancient fortress-city of Przemysl with its important road and rail junctions, then raced across the bridge over the San River and reached the city of Lvov and another major rail junction in a matter of days. Other contingents seized bridges over the Dvina River in the north and held them against Soviet counterattacks. In the south, a special battalion of Brandenburgers and Ukrainian nationalists, code-named Nightingale, infiltrated retreating Russian columns, hunting down NKVD security police and rescuing prominent Ukrainians slated for execution as potential collaborators. Brandenburgers in assault boats and gliders spearheaded a landing on a pair of islands off the coast of Estonia. All along the front, long-range reconnaissance platoons of Brandenburgers dressed in Soviet uniforms, with all papers in perfect order (even to letters from home), driving Soviet trucks, and headed by spokesmen conversing in fluent Russian, prowled hundreds of miles behind enemy lines.

At his headquarters in Berlin, Wilhelm Canaris followed the exploits of his men with fatherly pride. The fifty-four-year-old admiral was visibly thrilled that his young Brandenburgers were marching in the van of Germany's victorious armies, garnering more decorations and official commendations than virtually any other Wehrmacht unit. But the progress of the war, so

158

Using the trees as cover, two German commandos in mountain-troop uniforms battle Yugoslav partisans in the spring of 1943, when the Germans began using Brandenburgers as shock troops in the Balkans. For a while, their mobility and quickness made them more than a match for their elusive enemy.

satisfying from a military standpoint, was tearing him apart emotionally.

Every German triumph placed Canaris's esteem for his men and his passionate patriotism in direct conflict with a mounting dismay at the criminality of Hitler and his Nazi myrmidons. The admiral was a man of deeply rooted Christian values, and the destruction and mass slaughter that attended the German conquest of Poland had evoked a profound sense of personal and national guilt. It was even worse in the Soviet Union. The brutality that characterized Nazi policy in Russia filled him with horror and despair; he could not bear the knowledge that SS task forces following the combat troops were methodically hunting down and exterminating Jews, Bolsheviks, intellectuals, Russians, Ukrainians, and anyone else marked for death in Hitler's campaign of racial and political annihilation.

By the middle of 1941, the inner turmoil was taking an obvious toll on the Abwehr chief. "He made an old, tired, and war-weary impression," recalled an SS officer who met Canaris for the first time that August. With mounting concern, the admiral's staff watched him swing between apathy and supercharged emotion. The most trivial error by a subordinate was liable to provoke a response that verged on hysteria. Equally bewildering was his suddenly strange humor: Once while driving through Spain in an open touring car, Canaris spied a shepherd by the roadside and immediately ordered the auto halted, after which he rose to a standing position and gave the peasant his best formal military salute. When a puzzled companion inquired, "What is it, Excellency?" Canaris replied mysteriously, "You can never tell if there's a senior officer underneath."

Even the admiral's once-spruce appearance deteriorated. He often

turned up at his office with his uniform buttoned wrong and soiled with specks of food. Most alarming, his brilliant intellect seemed to be deserting him. The man who had once relished the mental exercise of conspiratorial plotting could no longer remember the details of individual operations.

Canaris's disintegration was not lost on his archrival, Reinhard Heydrich, chief of the RSHA, the umbrella organization that combined all of the police and intelligence functions of the SS. Heydrich saw the admiral's growing weakness as an opening to be exploited in the campaign to bring the

In June 1942, SS troops in Prague bear a wreath during a procession honoring Reinhard Heydrich, head of the Nazi intelligence service, and deputy Reich protector of Bohemia and Moravia. Heydrich's assassination cost the lives of over 1,400 innocent Czechs who were massacred by the Nazis in reprisal.

Abwehr to heel. In early 1942, Reinhard Heydrich met with Canaris and outlined a proposal in which a number of Abwehr counterintelligence functions would be taken over by the RSHA. To the horror of his staff, Canaris meekly acquiesced. Frantic string pulling on the part of Lieutenant Franz-Eccard von Bentivegni, head of the Abwehr's Section III, the counterespionage and counterintelligence division, temporarily blocked Heydrich's maneuver. But by spring, Abwehr authority had nonetheless been substantially undermined. Canaris traveled to Prague, where Heydrich, recently named deputy Reich protector of Bohemia and Moravia, had set up his new headquarters. On May 17, the two men signed a memorandum recognizing the RSHA's right to conduct a number of foreign intelligence operations that had once been the Abwehr's exclusive preserve.

Several days later, Heydrich's car was ambushed by a Czech assassination team organized by the British. Canaris immediately returned to Prague, but he never saw his old rival again. Heydrich died of his wounds on June 4. Canaris wept at the RSHA leader's funeral and later declared in a letter to Heydrich's widow that he had lost a "true friend." His grief was apparently genuine; on a personal level, he and Heydrich shared a deep love of music and had long been riding companions. But the savage Nazi reprisals for the killing could only have intensified Canaris's paralyzing moral dilemma. In one of the most notorious acts of the war, the entire town of Lidice was obliterated and its name expunged from all official records on the charge that its inhabitants had harbored the assassins. The 172 men and boys of the town were executed, while the women and small children were scattered around in various concentration camps. Another 1,200 citizens of Prague and Brno were slain in further retaliation for the death of Heydrich. More and more, Canaris was haunted by a single dreadful conviction: "God will pass judgment on us."

In the months that followed, the admiral's position was further undermined by a series of military debacles that exposed gaping deficiencies in the Abwehr's intelligence-gathering apparatus. In November 1942, Allied troops landed in North Africa, catching the German high command completely by surprise. "Canaris," stormed Alfred Jodl, chief of the Operations Staff, "has landed us in the soup." Jodl's bitter complaint was echoed by commanders on the eastern front, where the tide was steadily turning against the invaders. The longer the war went on and the farther the Germans advanced into the Soviet Union, the scantier and less reliable Abwehr reports became. "All we got from Canaris was rubbish," said one member of the Foreign Armies East command, and high command analysts steadily eroded Canaris's reputation. The evaluators would have been interested to know that by then the Abwehr's entire spy network within Great Britain had been detected and turned back on the Germans by British counterintelligence; the information reaching Berlin was only what the British wanted their enemy to know.

The admiral's decline was reflected in the fortunes of the Brandenburgers. Canaris had reserved the right to decide which Brandenburg units should be attached to which army group. But in the autumn of 1942, the Abwehr's special forces had been expanded to divisional strength, and Canaris was reduced to a mere adviser in their affairs. He was thus powerless to intervene when, in the defensive battles on the eastern front during the winter of 1942-43, Brandenburg units—lightly armed and ill equipped for protracted operations—were thrown into the brutal struggle. As a result, irreplaceable men trained to undertake the most complex intelligence operations were sacrificed as stopgap infantry reinforcements.

Canaris's tenuous position worsened in April 1943 with the arrest of two top Abwehr officers; the trumped-up charge was currency smuggling, but the real reason was evidence uncovered by the Gestapo that the officers were involved in military plots to overthrow Hitler. In the continuing investigation, other members of the Abwehr came under suspicion of treason. But that in itself was not necessarily enough to bring down Canaris. Conspiracy was a hallmark of the Third Reich, and there was scarcely a member of the Nazi hierarchy who was not aware of some sort of plot. But when suspicions of treachery were added to the failures of Abwehr intelligence, Canaris's downfall seemed inevitable.

No one was more keenly aware of that than Walter Schellenberg, chief of the RSHA's foreign intelligence section, Amt VI, and the most aggressively ambitious of Reinhard Heydrich's deputies. Schellenberg's personal relationship with Canaris was, if anything, even more amicable then Heydrich's had been. The older man appreciated Schellenberg's lively imagination and quick intelligence, and the younger man constantly professed his admiration for the Abwehr chief. But Schellenberg's ambitions left no room for a rival intelligence organization. Years earlier, he had drafted a detailed plan to create an integrated secret service by incorporating the Abwehr into his own Amt VI. After Heydrich's death, he persistently lobbied Reichsführer-SS Himmler to oust Canaris and implement the plan.

But Himmler was curiously reluctant to act. Unlike the generals, who by now were openly contemptuous of Canaris, Himmler retained a timid, almost superstitious respect for the Abwehr chief. And he seemed pathologically unwilling to broach the subject of Canaris to Hitler, long one of the admiral's greatest fans. Whenever Schellenberg offered newly incriminating information about Canaris, Himmler would nervously tap

After succeeding Reinhard Heydrich as chief of the SD in January 1943, Ernst Kaltenbrunner took up the fight to unseat Admiral Canaris and place the Abwehr under the control of the SS.

his thumbnail against his teeth and promise vaguely to bring the matter to Hitler's attention when the time was ripe. Schellenberg suspected that Himmler feared Canaris, for reasons unexplained. "I am certain that at some time or other Canaris must have got to know something incriminating against Himmler," Schellenberg later wrote, "for otherwise there is no possible explanation for Himmler's reaction to the material that I placed before him."

In January 1943, the impatient Schellenberg found an unexpected ally in the man chosen by Himmler to succeed Reinhard Heydrich as boss of the RSHA. He was Ernst Kaltenbrunner, head of the SS in Vienna. The appointment dumbfounded SS insiders. The new RSHA chief had neither the professional police qualifications nor the personal influence to account for his elevation to a position of such power. But Himmler had seen the power-hungry Heydrich as a threat to his own leadership and was determined not to make that mistake again; the unprepossessing Kaltenbrunner filled the bill perfectly. Moreover, Kaltenbrunner was a native of Linz, Hitler's hometown, and he worshiped the Führer with the sort of doglike devotion that was increasingly rare among the Nazi ruling class. In choosing the Austrian, Himmler scored a bull's-eye with Hitler, who, as Schellenberg dryly observed, "was convinced that this countryman of his had all the necessary qualifications for the job."

Schellenberg detested Kaltenbrunner on sight. "From the first moment, he made me feel quite sick," he later wrote, describing his new superior as a drunkard and lout with disgusting teeth and nicotine-stained hands that looked like those of an "old gorilla." Kaltenbrunner returned Schellenberg's loathing in full measure, accurately pegging the younger man as an opportunist whose sole loyalty was to his own career.

Yet despite their mutual antipathy, the two shared an overriding goal: the creation of a single German secret service under SS control. In fact, Kaltenbrunner had pressed for a unified intelligence service when Himmler first approached him about assuming Heydrich's old post—and he went straight to Himmler the moment he got a look at the Gestapo dossier on

Canaris. By then, "State Secret" documents on the admiral ran to several volumes attesting to Abwehr corruption, incompetence, and complicity in plots against the regime. Kaltenbrunner was as surprised as Schellenberg had been earlier when Himmler said mildly that he was well aware of the files, but that he had good reasons for not taking action.

Whatever those reasons were, the Reichsführer-SS could not ignore forever the obvious disintegration of Canaris's Abwehr. On January 23, 1943, the British Eighth Army took Tripoli in the first of a series of Allied victories that would culminate in the surrender of all German troops in Africa. On February 2, the Red Army recaptured Stalingrad. The OKW linked both disasters to intelligence failures.

Ultimately, the wily Himmler contrived what Schellenberg described as a "snowball tactic" to discredit the Abwehr chief in the eyes of the Führer. He never expressed his own opinion of Canaris to Hitler, but steadily encouraged the admiral's enemies to do so, while feeding them fresh bits of incriminating evidence to bolster their arguments.

Meanwhile, Schellenberg and Kaltenbrunner found another way to encroach on Abwehr territory. They raised their own Brandenburg-style force under Schellenberg's Amt VI, naming it the Oranienburg Special Training Course after the SS barracks at Oranienburg, fifteen miles north of Berlin. The special unit remained small at first; but by April 1943 its founders were emboldened to expand, and Kaltenbrunner found just the man to put in command: Captain Otto Skorzeny, a fellow Austrian and an old chum from his student days.

Skorzeny was a middle-class Viennese who had studied at the Vienna Technical College and then joined his father-in-law's engineering firm. He signed up with an SS motorized unit at the beginning of the war and was wounded in Russia in 1941. He had grown bored with duty as an SS tank instructor when Kaltenbrunner offered him a chance for action—and glory. Skorzeny saw it as a chance to "say good-bye to normal soldiering," and, as he later wrote, in accepting command of the unit he remembered the words of the philosopher Nietzsche: "Live dangerously!"

When Skorzeny took over, the Oranienburgers were already preparing for their first mission: cutting off the Allied supply routes to Russia through Iran by fomenting revolt among the Iranian mountain tribes near the Soviet border. A German officer had made contact with tribesmen who declared themselves only too happy to ambush Anglo-American supply columns in exchange for silver and the antique rifles and swords adorned with precious metals that they cherished as status symbols. Skorzeny plunged into preparations for the raid, dispatching his adjutant, Karl Radl, to scour Berlin's antique and gun shops for ancient fowling pieces and inlaid

muskets. But then he ran into the bureaucratic infighting that marred so many German operations: First the Luftwaffe refused to supply a transport for his parachutists; next, since the mission involved political considerations, control of the force in Iran was taken out of his hands and given to another agency. In any event, the operation amounted to little, and Skorzeny turned to another assignment, this one a pet project of Himmler's.

The SS chief wanted to launch a raid on the Soviet industrial town of Magnitogorsk, deep within the Ural Mountains, with the objective of destroying the city's blast furnaces and crippling its steel production. Skorzeny briskly began laying plans for the mission—only to conclude that it was unworkable. He was preparing a frank report to that effect when Schellenberg waylaid him with a cynical lesson in Nazi gamesmanship. "The more absurd the idea put to you by a really important person, the more rapturously you should welcome it," counseled the Amt VI chief. Schellenberg went on to advise a flurry of "showy preparations" and said, "Assurances must be incessantly given that operations are advancing apace." In time, he assured Skorzeny, Himmler's enthusiasm would wane, and he would eventually forget the whole idea.

Although this approach was at odds with his forthright nature, Skorzeny followed Schellenberg's advice. The months dragged by as he drilled his men and waited for something to happen. Then, on July 23, 1943, he was summoned to Hitler's East Prussian headquarters. A bold soldier was being sought to lead the Mussolini rescue team, and Himmler had suggested Skorzeny. As the Reichsführer-SS had hoped, Hitler was immediately taken with the powerful Austrian and gave him command of the operation.

The success of the Gran Sasso mission transformed the unknown captain overnight into one of Nazi Germany's most celebrated soldiers. And Adolf Hitler, who loved sensational coups, found the commando's brisk, can-do attitude a refreshing contrast to the gloom of his generals. Skorzeny proclaimed his philosophy: "It is never too late to start on something really important—it merely calls for speedier and more resolute action." Hitler liked that kind of thinking and rewarded Skorzeny with permission to expand the special forces greatly. Skorzeny was to have a separate battalion for every front on which the German army was engaged.

One of the few people immune to the Skorzeny magic was Wilhelm Canaris. Some weeks after his return from Italy, Skorzeny met with Canaris to announce that ten Brandenburg officers, most of them junior, wished to transfer to his command—and would Canaris kindly give his blessing? The newly promoted major, who was later described by an associate as "big, bold, and brave, but not all too bright," was no match for the Abwehr chief, who even in his decline could run intellectual circles around his

visitor. As Skorzeny later described the meeting, Canaris played an infuriating three-hour cat-and-mouse game with him. In the end, the admiral gave the impression that he had agreed. Then he refused to allow the transfer to go through. "He's like a jellyfish," Skorzeny fumed to his adjutant, Radl. "You can push your finger right through it and see it come out the other side, but when you've withdrawn it, the creature looks exactly the same as it did before." He added indignantly that such slippery behavior might be expected from an enemy, but that it was unspeakable "against another German!"

Skorzeny's feathers would not remain ruffled for long. He soon got his ten Brandenburgers—and more. Canaris's little diversion with him would prove to have been one of the master gamesman's last minor plays.

The situation in Italy that catapulted Skorzeny to fame also hastened the demise of the Abwehr. On July 29, just four days after Mussolini's fall, Canaris had flown to Venice to confer with General Cesare Amé, the head of Italian military intelligence. Canaris had been dispatched to discover whether or not Mussolini's successor, Pietro Badoglio, intended to fight on at Germany's side. Upon his return to Berlin, Canaris assured Hitler that Italy was the most faithful of allies.

It was a bald-faced lie. Amé had bluntly informed Canaris that Badoglio would conclude a separate peace with the Allies as soon as possible. The only thing holding Badoglio back was his fear that once the Germans got wind of an impending armistice, they would occupy Italy and nullify any treaty. Canaris, hoping that a quick Italian capitulation would hurry the end of the war, kept the truth to himself in order to lull Hitler and thus prevent a massing of German troops in Italy.

His ploy failed. Hitler mistrusted Badoglio and suspected Canaris's report from the first. Like his generals, he was getting fed up with Canaris's intelligence failures, and when Badoglio did sign an armistice with the Allies on September 3, he was ready to believe the Abwehr traitorous as well as useless. Only some fresh scandal was needed to convince him.

It happened in February 1944, when an important Abwehr operative in Istanbul defected to the British, compromising the German espionage apparatus in Turkey. Himmler was finally moved to condemn Canaris directly, suggesting to Hitler that the admiral's personal and professional failures had "risen to an intolerable level." Hitler angrily agreed and, on February 12, issued a curt directive ordering the creation of a "unified German secret information service." Canaris was unceremoniously retired, and Reichsführer-SS Himmler was placed in overall command. Himmler and Field Marshal Wilhelm Keitel, head of the armed forces high command,

At the Toplitzsee, the local gauleiter (right, in civilian dress) confers with officials from the Wehrmacht marine research station. The station's engineers suggested the lake as a dumping place for the Bernhard notes.

In July 1959, a diver adds a bundle of bogus British notes to those already found in the Toplitzsee. Spurred by rumors of sunken treasure, the German magazine Stern financed an effort that recovered a fraction of the cache.

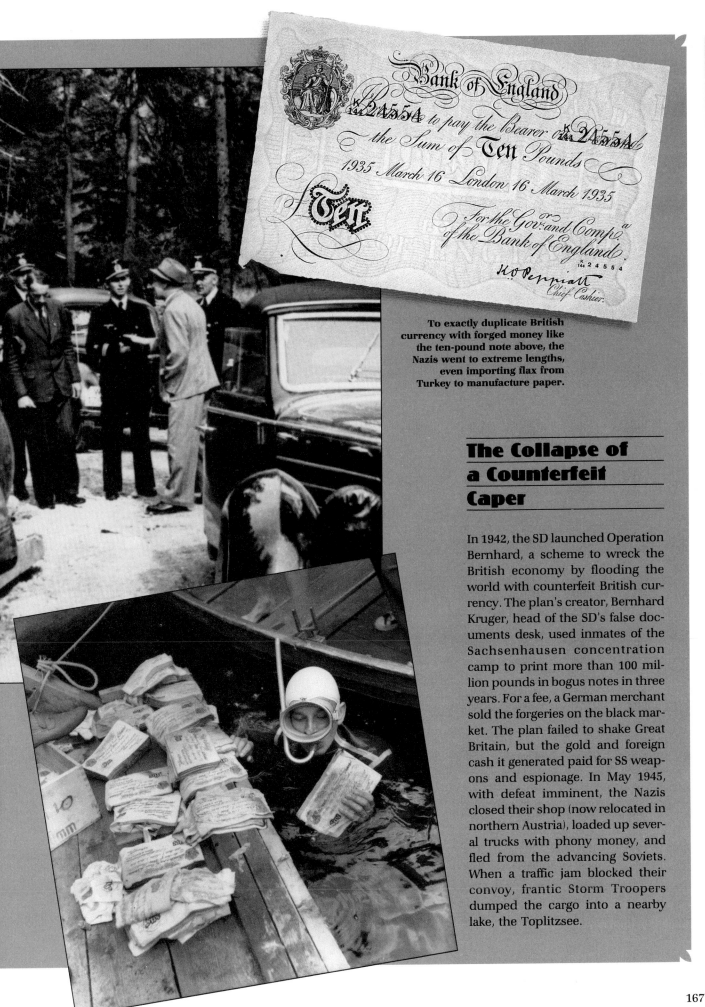

To exactly duplicate British currency with forged money like the ten-pound note above, the Nazis went to extreme lengths, even importing flax from Turkey to manufacture paper.

The Collapse of a Counterfeit Caper

In 1942, the SD launched Operation Bernhard, a scheme to wreck the British economy by flooding the world with counterfeit British currency. The plan's creator, Bernhard Kruger, head of the SD's false documents desk, used inmates of the Sachsenhausen concentration camp to print more than 100 million pounds in bogus notes in three years. For a fee, a German merchant sold the forgeries on the black market. The plan failed to shake Great Britain, but the gold and foreign cash it generated paid for SS weapons and espionage. In May 1945, with defeat imminent, the Nazis closed their shop (now relocated in northern Austria), loaded up several trucks with phony money, and fled from the advancing Soviets. When a traffic jam blocked their convoy, frantic Storm Troopers dumped the cargo into a nearby lake, the Toplitzsee.

were ordered to work out between them how to carve up the Abwehr.

Schellenberg and Kaltenbrunner had counted on having Canaris's service transferred intact to them as a new military section of the RSHA. The OKW, however, insisted on having front-line intelligence and counterespionage units allotted to the Wehrmacht. The dickering continued into the summer. In the end, Keitel wound up with the Abwehr's Section III and Canaris's original battlefield intelligence section, and Schellenberg won all the rest of the Abwehr functions, which were combined into a single Military Office attached to his Amt VI.

Schellenberg did not get the Brandenburgers, however. Two days before Hitler issued the order dismantling Canaris's organization, the Brandenburg Division was removed from Section II and subordinated directly to the Wehrmacht. But this was not as great a loss to Schellenberg as it once might have been. The Brandenburg had changed drastically. Brought back up to strength with new recruits following its devastating casualties in Russia, it was no longer a pure special forces unit. The change in character was emphasized in 1944 by a reorganization that split the division into separate combat units and so-called *Streif Korps*—"raiding corps"—which were trained for special missions. Skorzeny, authorized to recruit wherever he pleased, wound up with 900 Streif Korps members, giving the SS the cream of what remained of the old Brandenburgers.

Yet Skorzeny's special forces never quite achieved the overall military effectiveness of the early Brandenburgers. Part of the problem was the personality of their leader. For all his courage and élan (or perhaps because

In a burst of inventiveness fueled by Germany's desperate military plight, Nazi engineers churned out some fantastic secret weaponry in the final year of the war. A crew on board a German naval vessel lowers a manned torpedo, called a *Neger*, into the sea *(above)*. The pilot of a Neger sat in a modified torpedo casing and, after using the vertical rod in front of him to sight his target, fired a live torpedo slung below. A Plexiglas dome protected the vessel and its occupant from ocean waves, but the Negers were not submersible. Although the *Biber* midget submarine *(opposite)* was designed like a U-boat and could dive ninety feet, it could not cruise underwater and had to fire its two torpedoes from the surface. This one-man vessel was used primarily off the coast of Holland to attack Allied shipping.

of it), Skorzeny was not a good leader on a grand scale. He was interested in action, not in organizational details, and it was far easier for him to focus on a single exciting mission than on overall special forces strategy and operations. "He was the ideal man to lead any raid or foray," observed Wilhelm Hoettl, an SS intelligence officer. "A lone fighter and Storm Trooper par excellence, but no divisional commander."

Moreover, Hitler and Himmler exacerbated the situation by forever treating Skorzeny as a kind of personal, all-purpose secret weapon, sending him

off on special missions at the expense of his broad command. His first assignment after rescuing Mussolini was to kidnap Marshal Philippe Pétain, on the theory that the president of Vichy France was contemplating a switch of allegiance to the Allied side. After assembling two SS rifle battalions, a group of policemen, and three companies of infantry for the mission and skulking around Paris for days waiting for the signal to begin, Skorzeny was abruptly called back to Germany. The Reich's Foreign Office and its security and military headquarters could not agree on whether the mission was advisable.

Later, in the spring of 1944, Skorzeny was ordered to organize another kidnapping—this time of Yugoslavia's partisan leader, Marshal Josip Broz Tito. After making a bold reconnaissance deep into partisan territory accompanied only by two sergeants and armed with a single machine gun, Skorzeny was ready to proceed—but learned at the last minute that the army's X Corps had already sched-

uled a massive airborne raid on Tito's headquarters. Skorzeny sat out the assault, which resulted in heavy German casualties and netted nothing more than one of Tito's uniforms.

That fall, the Führer had yet another job for his favorite commando. On September 10, Skorzeny was summoned before Hitler, who bitterly outlined the worsening situation in the east. In addition to the threat posed by the onrushing Red Army, the Führer faced the mass desertion of his allies. In July, Rumania had abruptly switched sides and had declared war on Germany. Now it appeared that Admiral Nicholas von Horthy, regent of Hungary, was about to follow suit and seek a separate peace with the Allies. "So you, Skorzeny," said the Führer, fixing the major with burning eyes, "must be prepared to seize the citadel of Budapest by force, if Horthy betrays his alliance to us."

A few days later, Skorzeny appeared in Budapest dressed in civilian clothes and carrying a dog-eared Baedeker. Posing as "Dr. Wolf" from Cologne, he took up residence at a modest hotel and began to play the tourist. Over the next few days, Dr. Wolf took particular interest in the Burgberg, the fortified mount that was the seat of the Hungarian government and the site of Horthy's residence. He also surreptitiously got in touch with the local Gestapo for the latest information on Horthy's activities. He soon learned that the aging admiral's son, also named Nicholas but nicknamed Niki, had contacted Yugoslav partisans to act as intermediaries in negotiating Hungary's surrender to the Russians.

Niki Horthy was a notorious playboy, for whom his indulgent father had a well-known weak spot. Skorzeny decided that the simplest way to keep Admiral Horthy in line would be to take his son hostage. Skorzeny's special forces had already arrived in the area and were billeted outside Budapest. On October 15, the day Niki was scheduled to meet with his partisan contacts, the Germans, under the command of Skorzeny's Chief of Staff Adrian von Fölkersam, slipped into position in the streets around the house where the meeting was to take place. It was a clear, sparkling autumn morning. The square just outside the house was empty except for a Hungarian military truck and Niki's car.

Then Dr. Wolf drove into the square. He parked in front of the two vehicles, got out of his car, and pretended to tinker with its engine. Moments later, a pair of German MPs strolled by, apparently on routine patrol. Suddenly, they dropped their casual air and dashed toward the house. The response was instant. Hungarian soldiers inside the truck opened fire with a machine gun. One of the Germans fell, and Skorzeny darted out and dragged him by the collar to safety behind his car. As Hungarian soldiers streamed into the square, two other Germans who had been loitering

In the aftermath of a failed kidnapping mission, German soldiers display a uniform belonging to Marshal Tito, leader of Yugoslavia's Communist Resistance, at his headquarters near a small Bosnian town in May 1944. Tito himself escaped to Italy after a fierce fight between his partisans and German troops who had dropped by parachute and glider.

nearby started firing back. "By then my car was not much more than a sieve," recalled Skorzeny. "Bullets ricocheting from walls passed unpleasantly near, and we could only put our noses out of cover long enough to take potshots at the enemy."

Then Skorzeny heard Fölkersam's men running up the street. The SS detachment stormed into the square, overpowering the Hungarians. The battle was over in less than five minutes. Skorzeny and his men dashed into the house to find Niki Horthy already in the custody of Germans who had hidden themselves in the building earlier that day. Young Horthy was beside himself, shrieking vituperation at his captors, who finally shut him up by rolling him in a carpet and securing it with a length of curtain cord. Thus concealed, the regent's son was hauled out to a waiting truck and driven off to be put on a plane to Vienna.

Skorzeny did not have long to wait for Admiral Horthy's reaction. That afternoon, Radio Budapest cut into its regular programming for a speech by the head of state. Far from caving in, Horthy launched into a furious tirade against the Germans, after which he declared that he had already drawn up a provisional armistice; hostilities with the Russians would cease immediately.

Skorzeny's only recourse now was a direct attack on the Burgberg. He moved swiftly, gambling that the events of the last few hours had created enough confusion to enable him to achieve his objective without a full-scale battle. At three o'clock the next morning, he headed to his command post at the foot of the Burgberg. Gulping down a cup of coffee, he outlined his plan to Fölkersam and the other officers, and at 6:00 a.m., an SS column accompanied by two Panther tanks started up the hill.

Leading the way in a jeep, Skorzeny passed Hungarian sentries along the way, who, as he had hoped, stood back and offered no resistance. As the column approached Horthy's fortified residence, three Hungarian tanks reacted similarly, raising their cannons to signal that they would not fire. Suddenly, Skorzeny stood up and waved his arm at one of his Panthers. The tank surged past and smashed through the barricade surrounding the residence. Skorzeny's men poured through the opening and into the building. The firefight that followed lasted only a few minutes. In a satisfying reprise of the Mussolini mission, Skorzeny's men quickly overwhelmed Horthy's guards and took the admiral prisoner.

Admiral Horthy was taken under guard to Germany, where he sat out the rest of the war as a "guest" of the Führer. A pro-German puppet was

Stepping over surrendered weapons, German troops search the grounds of the Burgberg, Budapest's royal palace, after their lightning raid in October 1944 that resulted in the kidnapping of Niki Horthy, son of the Hungarian regent. Shocked Hungarian soldiers guarding the palace offered little resistance.

Upon learning in September 1944 that the Hungarian regent, Admiral Nicholas von Horthy (*opposite*), was negotiating with Axis enemies for a separate peace, Adolf Hitler ordered Otto Skorzeny to prevent the capitulation. "He is approaching both the Western powers and the Russians," the Führer raged. "He is even prepared to throw himself on the mercy of the Kremlin."

installed in his place, and the Hungarians continued to fight the Russians.

On October 21, Skorzeny was back at Hitler's headquarters to bask once again in the Führer's gratitude. Hitler promoted him to lieutenant colonel, decorated him yet again—this time awarding the German Cross in gold—then took him by the hand to a secluded corner and asked him to recount the operation, detail by detail.

After Skorzeny had at last satisfied his rapt audience of one, he rose to take his leave. But Hitler drew him back down. "Don't go, Skorzeny," he said. "I am now going to give you the most important job of your life." He paused, then raced on, his voice rising. "In December, Germany will commence a great offensive that may well decide its fate." Over the next few hours, he outlined the details of a counterattack in the west, a massive strike by three German armies at the center of the American and British forces. Skorzeny would lead a brigade dressed in captured American uniforms and driving captured American vehicles. His men would plunge straight through the Allied lines, sowing terror and confusion as they went. "The world thinks Germany is finished, with only the day and hour of the funeral to be appointed," raged Hitler. "I am going to show them how mistaken they are. The corpse will rise and hurl itself in fury against the West. Then we shall see."

For all their Führer's passion that evening in the fall of 1944, most of Germany's generals—and the more pragmatic of the Nazis—knew that the war had been lost. On June 6, when Allied invasion forces landed in Normandy, the initiative had irretrievably gone over to the enemy in the west as well as in the east; a counterattack in the west could only prolong the agony. And a desire to make peace before Germany was destroyed by armies driving in on all sides gave fresh impetus to the plots swirling around Hitler. In the previous year, the dictator had escaped at least three assassination attempts. On July 20, he survived yet another—a military-backed bomb plot to blow him to oblivion in his Wolf's Lair headquarters.

The scheme had narrowly failed, and in the ferocious Gestapo manhunts and investigations that followed, the name of Wilhelm Canaris was prominent among those suspected of involvement in the conspiracy. And so it was that on July 23, a pleasant Sunday afternoon, Walter Schellenberg drove to Canaris's home on the outskirts of Berlin. The former Abwehr chief guessed immediately why his one-time colleague had come. "Somehow," he said quietly, "I felt it would be you."

Canaris went upstairs, changed clothes, and packed a small valise. As he prepared to leave, he looked slowly and sadly around, then put his arm across the younger man's shoulders as they walked out to the car.

They drove fifty miles to the Security Police academy at Fürstenberg an der Havel. There, about twenty senior officers who had been arrested in connection with the plot were being held under guard before being sent to the Gestapo's dungeons in the Prinz-Albrecht-Strasse headquarters in Berlin. Canaris asked Schellenberg to stay awhile, and the two men had supper together, sharing a bottle of red wine and chatting about old times. Evidently hoping that Himmler would intervene to protect him one last time, Canaris asked Schellenberg to arrange a meeting with the SS chief. When Schellenberg finally left at about eleven, Canaris warned him to steer clear of the kind of trouble he himself was now in and gave him a final embrace. "You are my only hope," he said with tears in his eyes. "Good-bye, young friend." They would never see one another again.

Schellenberg later claimed that he did speak with Himmler and that the SS chief had visited Canaris. But even if Himmler had been so inclined, it was too late to save the little admiral. Although Gestapo sleuths and interrogators found no evidence directly tying Canaris to the July 20 plot, his long association with the conspirators was enough to seal his doom.

On February 7, 1945, Canaris was sent to Flossenbürg concentration camp, near the Czech border. There, as the prisoner code-named Caesar by his jailers, the admiral was handcuffed and shackled by the ankles to the wall of cell 22. He was freed of his fetters only for short walks in the

In February 1945, Colonel Otto Skorzeny chats with his men on the eastern front. The spirit of his troops in the final battles with the Soviets was so impressive that British radio—the BBC—reported inaccurately that he had been promoted to major general and entrusted by Hitler with the defense of Berlin.

prison yard—and for further interrogation. At about ten o'clock on the evening of April 8, the prisoner next-door in cell 21 heard Canaris being led back from yet another session with his inquisitors. Soon after, he heard tapping on the cell wall; it was Canaris sending a message in the Morse-like code devised by Flossenbürg's inmates. "Nose broken at last interrogation," Canaris is remembered as having signaled. "My time is up. Was not a traitor. Did my duty as a German. If you survive, remember me to my wife."

Shortly after dawn the next morning, April 9, the fifty-eight-year-old Canaris was marched naked and barefoot to a crude gallows. He mounted a small stepladder. A noose was placed around his neck, and the stepladder was knocked away.

"The little admiral took a very long time," related a witness to many such events. "He was jerked up and down once or twice." An SS doctor had the decency to say, "Admiral Canaris died a staunch and manly death." ✚

A Covert
Mission on the
Ghost Front

In late July 1944, as Allied armies swept eastward from the beaches of Normandy, Adolf Hitler conceived a bold scheme, destined to be Germany's last major counteroffensive of the war, aimed at retrieving his country's fortunes on the western front. The plan, code-named Watch on the Rhine and resulting in the conflict known as the Battle of the Bulge, called for a massive blitzkrieg-style attack in the rugged Ardennes region of Belgium and Luxembourg, a sector so quiet that American forces called it the Ghost Front.

By launch date, December 16, 300,000 German soldiers had been massed opposite the unsuspecting Americans. Most of the divisions earmarked for the assault were elite panzer troops whose armored columns were expected to pierce the enemy lines, cross the Meuse River, and capture the Belgian port city of Antwerp, 100 miles in the Allied rear.

In addition to conventional forces, the gambit in the Ardennes would include a newly organized 2,500-man unit—Panzerbrigade 150—to be led by SS Colonel Otto Skorzeny, the Third Reich's most successful commando officer, on a top-secret mission called Operation

Greif, or Operation Griffin. The three battle groups in Panzerbrigade 150—armed and equipped with captured American uniforms and vehicles—would follow in the wake of the main German onslaught, then branch off on side roads, spreading confusion through the Allied defenders and seizing the strategic bridges over the Meuse.

The most daring and dangerous assignment of Operation Griffin fell to 160 volunteers selected for their proficiency in the English language. Working in teams of three to four men, clad in GI uniforms and driving American jeeps, they would infiltrate Allied lines in advance of the German panzer units. At Skorzeny's training camp near the Bavarian town of Grafenwöhr, these "Griffin Commandos" were given a crash course in covert operations and conditioned to think, speak, and act like American GIs.

Operation Griffin was successful in its early stages—success that could be attributed as much to good luck as to the courage and skill of the commandos. But although its initial achievements augured well for its final outcome, the undertaking was ultimately a failure.

Wearing captured American uniforms, a squad of Skorzeny's men trains for Operation Griffin. One commando called the training "more intense and concentrated than anything any of us had gone through before."

Transforming Germans into GIs

Isolated from their comrades in the Grafenwöhr training camp and forbidden to write home, the English-speaking commando contingent of Panzerbrigade 150 underwent a rigorous regimen that included athletics, hand-to-hand combat, target practice, and instruction in the use of American weapons and plastic explosives.

Hollywood films, particularly war movies, were used to help the German soldiers master American slang and body language. The traditionally rigid German military bearing was abandoned, and Skorzeny's men were encouraged to chew gum, slouch with their hands in their pockets, and salute their officers in a casual fashion. Some commandos visited captive Americans in prisoner-of-war camps to perfect their impersonations of GIs. When they were judged ready to undertake the mission, each of the volunteers received an American uniform, false identity papers, and rolls of counterfeit dollars.

The Griffin Commandos were grimly realistic about their dangerous enterprise. Wearing enemy uniforms in covert operations violated international rules of war and in fact was punishable by death. The German high command expected few commandos to survive the mission, and each man's kit included a suicide tablet.

With only two captured American tanks available to them, Skorzeny's men were forced to make do with German Panthers camouflaged with American markings *(right)*. Skorzeny said, "They can deceive only very young American troops, viewed at night, from very far away!"

Soldiers of Panzerbrigade 150 train in an American half-track personnel carrier *(opposite, below)*, one of some two dozen captured vehicles that were loaned to Operation Griffin.

A group of German commandos outfitted as Americans take time-out from their rigorous training schedule. "It was fantastic to see this mob of familiar soldiers changed into GIs," one volunteer recalled, "so improbable and uncanny."

Behind Enemy Lines in Disguise

The Ardennes offensive got under way at 5:15 a.m. on December 16, 1944. "A truly hellish spectacle sprang to life," one Griffin Commando remembered. "Hundreds of blinding searchlights pointed long white fingers at the American positions, and from the background where the artillery and rocket launchers stood, there was a fireworks display such as we had never seen before." Hastily discarding the paratrooper overalls that concealed their GI uniforms, Skorzeny's commandos started up their American jeeps and moved forward in the wake of the advancing armored columns.

Although the Allied defenders gave way before the sudden onslaught, Skorzeny's plans began to go awry as the bulk of Panzerbrigade 150 was stuck in a massive traffic jam of tanks and armored vehicles. When Allied resistance stiffened, Skorzeny's brigade found itself caught up in the fighting. Unable to carry out his mission, on the second day of the offensive the commando chief decided to call off Operation Griffin and consolidate his three battle groups into a traditional army unit. But by that time seven jeeps carrying Griffin Commando teams were behind American lines, headed for the bridges across the Meuse River and their ultimate objective.

At the start of the Ardennes offensive, SS panzer troops from the battle group commanded by Lieut. Colonel Joachim Peiper move past a wrecked American vehicle in the battle-scarred village of Honsfeld.

Driving American trucks, Skorzeny's commandos enter the snow-covered Blanken-heimer Forest, staging area for the December 16 offensive.

A German half-track bearing American insignia burns in Regné, Belgium, after being knocked out by American fire.

An American soldier examines a damaged Sherman tank abandoned by Panzerbrigade 150 during the Ardennes battle.

The Breakdown of a Bold Masquerade

Despite Skorzeny's plans, fewer than thirty of his commandos actually managed to infiltrate the American defenses. Initially apprehensive that they would be recognized, the Germans soon discovered that the chaos behind the Allied lines worked to their advantage. "We realized with increasing satisfaction that our disguise was fairly complete," one commando recalled, "and accordingly felt more and more safe."

When their jeeps were stopped at United States checkpoints, the member of a commando team who was the most fluent in English would speak for the rest of the group, usually explaining that they had been cut off by the German attack and were attempting to rejoin their retreating units. As they headed west for the Meuse, the commandos did what damage they could, cutting telephone lines, removing road signs, and waylaying isolated Allied couriers.

But the phony GIs soon found that they had made several fatal errors. They traveled four men to a jeep and at night kept their headlights covered to stay inconspicuous—in noticeable contrast to American practice. These mistakes, coupled with tightened security by nervous Allied forces, resulted in the capture of at least two commando teams. None of the remaining teams was able to reach the Meuse.

Wary GIs watch as a commando captured from Operation Griffin removes the American clothing he wore over his own uniform.

A dead German soldier, partly clad in GI uniform, lies beside a bullet-riddled American jeep. Wehrmacht troops caught with United States gear were frequently shot on the spot by jittery American soldiers.

On December 17, American MPs manning a checkpoint at the town of Aywaille apprehended three German infiltrators who were unable to give the correct password. Within a week, Griffin Commandos Günther Billing, Manfred Pernass, and Wilhelm Schmidt had been tried and sentenced to death as spies—a punishment due in part to Schmidt's claim that their mission included the capture of General Eisenhower. The execution took place just after dawn on December 23 at a barracks in Henri-Chapelle, Belgium. The men were bound and blindfolded, and white disks were affixed to their chests to serve as targets (*above*). Just before the firing squad pulled their triggers, Billing shouted, "Long live our Führer, Adolf Hitler!" At least three other commandos died in Operation Griffin—shot on the spot as they were apprehended.

Acknowledgments and Picture Credits

The editors thank: Austria: Innsbruck—Günter Peis. England: London—Terry Charman, Paul Kemp, Allan Williams, Mike Willis, Imperial War Museum; Peter Elliott, Royal Air Force Museum; Brian Johnson. France: Paris—Christian Bricoud, Photothèque, Éditions Hachette; Jean-Paul Pallud. Germany: Babenhausen—Heinz Nowarra. Bad Säckingen—Renée Wagner. Berlin—Heidi Klein, Bildarchiv Preussischer Kulturbesitz; Wolfgang Streubel, Ullstein Bilderdienst. Eching-Ammersee—Helmut Spaeter. Grosshansdorf—Heinz Höhne. Koblenz—Meinrad Nilges, Bundesarchiv. Munich—Elisabeth Heidt, Süddeutscher Verlag Bilderdienst. Rösrath-Hoffnungsthal—Helga Müller. United States: Alabama—Farley L. Berman. Arizona—Dr. Bruce Saunders. District of Columbia—Stuart L. Butler, Robin E. Cookson, Terri Hammett, John E. Taylor, Jim Trimble, National Archives; Larry Wilson, Smithsonian Institution. Louisiana—Keith Melton. Maryland—Earl J. Coates, David Gaddy, Thomas Roers, National Security Agency; Bruce Frederic Blackburn. New Jersey—Jim Phillips. New York—Todd Gustavson, Pat Musolf, George Eastman House. Pennsylvania—Dr. William White, NiTech Research Corporation.

Credits from left to right are separated by semicolons, from top to bottom by dashes. Cover: Private collection. 4: Süddeutscher Verlag Bilderdienst, Munich; Otto Wagner, Bad Säckingen. 5: Ullstein Bilderdienst, Berlin. 6: Bildarchiv Preussischer Kulturbesitz (BPK), Berlin—Ullstein Bilderdienst, Berlin—ADN-Zentralbild, Berlin. 7: Ullstein Bilderdienst, Berlin. 8: Günter-Peis-Archiv, Innsbruck. 9: Bundesarchiv, Koblenz. 10: Süddeutscher Verlag Bilderdienst, Munich—Ullstein Bilderdienst, Berlin. 11: AP Bilderdienst, Frankfurt. 12: Bettmann Newsphotos, New York. 15: Ullstein Bilderdienst, Berlin. 17: BPK, Berlin. 20, 21: Süddeutscher Verlag Bilderdienst, Munich. 22, 23: Bill van Calsem, courtesy Keith Melton. 24, 25: UPI/Bettmann, New York. 27: Ullstein Bilderdienst, Berlin. 29: Süddeutscher Verlag Bilderdienst, Munich. 31: Otto Hagel for LIFE—Wide World Photos, New York. 32, 33: Otto Hagel for LIFE (2); Wide World Photos, New York. 34, 35: Bettmann Newsphotos, New York—Wide World Photos, New York. 36, 37: Günter-Peis-Archiv, Innsbruck. 38, 39: Ullstein Bilderdienst, Berlin—from *Der Zweite Weltkrieg* by Klaus Scheel, Pahl-Rugenstein Verlag, Cologne, 1952. 40, 41: Andreas Feininger for LIFE, inset Wide World Photos, New York. 42, 43: Bettmann Newsphotos, New York. 44: Wide World Photos, New York, inset Bettmann Newsphotos—Federal Bureau of Investigation (FBI); Wide World Photos, New York—from *Hitler's Spies* by David Kahn, Hodder and Stoughton, London, 1978. 46: Wide World Photos, New York. 47: FBI—Bernard Hoffman for LIFE—FBI. 48: Bettmann Newsphotos, New York. 49: Bettmann Newsphotos, insets Wide World Photos, New York (2)—FBI (2). 50: Wide World Photos, New York; Bettmann Newsphotos, New York—Wide World Photos, New York; Bettmann Newsphotos, New York. 51: Wide World Photos, New York. 52: Archiv J. Piekalkiewicz, Rösrath-Hoffnungsthal. 54, 55: FBI (3); UPI (2); FBI (3). 56: FBI. 57: Günter-Peis-Archiv, Innsbruck. 58, 59: National Archives microfilm #T77 1521. 61: FBI; Bettmann Newsphotos, New York. 62: Bill van Calsem, courtesy Keith Melton. 64, 65: Wide World Photos, New York; Bettmann Newsphotos. 66-67: Bettmann Newsphotos. 68, 69: Bill van Calsem, courtesy Keith Melton. 71: Günter-Peis-Archiv, Innsbruck. 72-77: Archiv J. Piekalkiewicz, Rösrath-Hoffnungsthal. 78: From *Hitler's Secret War in South America 1939-1945* by Stanley E. Hilton, Louisiana State University Press, Baton Rouge, 1981. 80, 81: *La Prensa*, Buenos Aires, Argentina (2); inset, National Archives. 83: Günter-Peis-Archiv, Innsbruck. 85: From *Arrows of the Almighty* by Michael Bar-Zohar, Macmillan, New York, 1985. 86, 87: Süddeutscher Verlag Bilderdienst, Munich; from *The Service* by Reinhard Gehlen, World Publishing, New York, 1972. 88: George Rodger for LIFE. 89: From *Operation Condor* by John W. Eppler, MacDonald and Jane's, London, 1978; courtesy John Eppler. 90, 91: Courtesy John Eppler—from *The Cat and the Mice* by Leonard Mosley, Harper & Brothers Publishing, New York, 1958; Bob Landry for LIFE. 92: George Rodger for LIFE. 93: Imam/Dar al-Hilal. 94, 95: From *Operation Condor* by John W. Eppler, MacDonald and Jane's, London, 1978—Ahmad Soliman/Dar al-Hilal; from *The Cat and the Mice* by Leonard Mosley, Harper & Brothers Publishing, New York, 1958 (2). 96, 97: Dr. William White; National Archives RG 373. 98, 99: Heinz Nowarra, Babenhausen—Hanfried Schliephake, Königsbrunn; Pilot Press, Bromley, Kent, U.K.—Barbara Puorro Galasso, International Museum of Photography at George Eastman House, Rochester, New York; Pilot Press, Bromley, Kent, U.K. 100, 101: Bundesarchiv, Koblenz (2); National Archives RG 373. 102, 103: From *World War II Photo Intelligence* by Roy M. Stanley II, Charles Scribner's Sons, New York, 1981—Süddeutscher Verlag Bilderdienst, Munich; Bundesarchiv, Koblenz; National Archives RG 373. 104, 105: Süddeutscher Verlag Bilderdienst, Munich; National Archives RG 373. 106, 107: National Archives RG 373. 108: BPK, Berlin. 110, 111: Dutch Archive for War Documentation, Riod. 112: From *Colonel Henri's Story* by Hugo Bleicher, William Kimber, London, 1954. 114, 115: Archiv J. Piekalkiewicz, Rösrath-Hoffnungsthal. 117, 118: Robert Marshall Collection, London. 121: Jelte Rep, Van Holkema & Warendorf. 122-125: Dutch State Archive for War Documentation, Riod. 127: Smithsonian Institution 25157AC. 130, 132: Archiv J. Piekalkiewicz, Rösrath-Hoffnungsthal. 133: From *The Red Orchestra* by Gilles Perrault, Simon and Schuster, New York, 1967. 134: From *Geheime Reichssache 330* by Heinz Schroter, Eduard Kaiser Verlag, Klagenfurt, 1969. 135: From *The Red Orchestra* by Gilles Perrault, Simon and Schuster, New York, 1967. 136: Archiv J. Piekalkiewicz, Rösrath-Hoffnungsthal. 138-140: Larry Sherer, courtesy National Security Agency (NSA), Fort Meade, Md. 141: Artwork by William J. Hennessy, Jr. 142: Brian Johnson. 143: Larry Sherer, courtesy NSA, Fort Meade, Md.—Larry Sherer, courtesy Don Mindemann. 144: From *Enigma* by Wladyslaw Kozaczuk, University Publications of America, Frederick, Md., 1984. 145: From *The Enigma War* by Jozef Garlinski, Charles Scribner's Sons, New York, 1979 (2)—Larry Sherer, courtesy NSA, Fort Meade, Md. 146: From *Top Secret Ultra* by Peter Calvocoressi, Cassell, London, 1980—Brian Johnson—from *The Enigma War* by Jozef Garlinski, Charles Scribner's Sons, New York, 1979. 147: NSA Museum of Cryptography, Fort Meade, Md. 148: Imperial War Museum, London. 150: Bundesarchiv, Koblenz. 154, 155: Otto Wagner, Bad Säckingen, Innsbruck. 156: Günter-Peis-Archiv; except top right from *Getarnt Getäusche und doch Getreu: Die geheimnisvollen Brandenburger* by Herbert Kriegsheim, Bernard & Graefe, Berlin, 1958. 159: S.I.R.P./E.C.P Armées, Paris. 160: Camera Press, London. 163: Robert Hunt Library, London. 166, 167: Stern-Archiv, Hamburg (2); Bill van Calsem, courtesy Keith Melton. 168: Robert Hunt Library, London. 169: Imperial War Museum, London. 171: Museum of Revolution of Bosnia and Herzegovina, Sarajevo. 172: ADN-Zentralbild, Berlin. 173: Bundesarchiv, Koblenz. 175: ADN-Zentralbild, Berlin. 176-179: Archiv J. Piekalkiewicz, Rösrath-Hoffungsthal. 180: Courtesy Jean-Paul Pallud. 181: Bundesarchiv, Koblenz—National Archives 111-SC-199641—Archiv J. Piekalkiewicz, Rösrath-Hoffungsthal. 182, 183: National Archives 111-SC-199446, 111-SC-198678. 184, 185: Süddeutscher Verlag Bilderdienst, Munich—Associated Press.

Bibliography

Books

Bar-Zohar, Michael, *Arrows of the Almighty: The Most Extraordinary True Spy Story of World War II.* New York: Macmillan, 1985.

Bleicher, Hugo, *Colonel Henri's Story.* Ed. by Ian Colvin. London: William Kimber, 1954.

Breuer, William, *Hitler's Undercover War: The Nazi Espionage Invasion of the U.S.A.* New York: St. Martin's Press, 1989.

Brissaud, André, *The Nazi Secret Service.* Transl. by Milton Waldman. London: The Bodley Head, 1974.

Brookes, Andrew J., *Photo Reconnaissance.* London: Ian Allan, 1975.

Dasch, George J., *Eight Spies against America.* New York: Robert M. McBride, 1959.

Diamond, Sander A., *The Nazi Movement in the United States 1924-1941.* Ithaca, N.Y.: Cornell University Press, 1974.

Eppler, John, *Operation Condor: Rommel's Spy.* Transl. by S. Seago. London: Macdonald and Jane's, 1977.

Farago, Ladislas, *The Game of the Foxes: The Untold Story of German Espionage in the United States and Great Britain during World War II.* New York: David McKay, 1971.

Foot, M. R. D., *SOE in France: An Account of the Work of the British Special Operations Executive in France 1940-1944.* Frederick, Md.: University Publications of America, 1984.

Gehlen, Reinhard, *The Service: The Memoirs of General Reinhard Gehlen.* Transl. by David Irving. New York: World Publishing, 1972.

Giskes, H. J., *London Calling North Pole.* New York: The British Book Centre, 1953.

Haldane, R. A., *The Hidden War.* New York: St. Martin's Press, 1978.

Hilton, Stanley E., *Hitler's Secret War in South America 1939-1945.* Baton Rouge: Louisiana State University Press, 1981.

Hoettl, Wilhelm, *The Secret Front: The Story of Nazi Political Espionage.* Transl. by R. H. Stevens. New York: Frederick A. Praeger, 1954.

Höhne, Heinz:
Canaris. Transl. by J. Maxwell Brownjohn. Garden City, N.Y.: Doubleday, 1979.
Codeword: Direktor. Transl. by Richard Barry. New York: Coward, McCann & Geoghegan, 1971.
The Order of the Death's Head: The Story of Hitler's S.S. Transl. by Richard Barry. New York: Coward-McCann, 1970.

Höhne, Heinz, and Hermann Zolling, *The General Was a Spy: The Truth about General Gehlen and His Spy Ring.* New York: Coward, McCann & Geoghegan, 1972.

Kahn, David:
The Codebreakers: The Story of Secret Writing. New York: Macmillan, 1967.
Hitler's Spies: German Military Intelligence in World War II. London: Hodder and Stoughton, 1978.

Kelso, Nicholas, *Errors of Judgement: SOE's Disaster in the Netherlands, 1941-1944.* London: Robert Hale, 1988.

Ladd, James D., Keith Melton, and Peter Mason, *Clandestine Warfare: Weapons and Equipment of the SOE and OSS.* London: Blandford Press, 1988.

Leverkuehn, Paul, *German Military Intelligence.* Transl. by R. H. Stevens and Constantine FitzGibbon. London: Weidenfeld and Nicolson, 1954.

Lorain, Pierre, *Clandestine Operations: The Arms and Techniques of the Resistance, 1941-1944.* Transl. by David Kahn. New York: Macmillan, 1972.

Lucas, James:
Germany's Elite Panzer Force: Grossdeutschland. London: Macdonald and Jane's, 1979.
Kommando: German Special Forces of World War Two. London: Arms and Armour Press, 1985.

Masterman, J. C., *The Double-Cross System in the War of 1939 to 1945.* New Haven, Conn.: Yale University Press, 1972.

Mendelsohn, John, ed., *Covert Warfare.* New York: Garland Publishing, 1989.

Miller, Marvin D., *Wunderlich's Salute.* Smithtown, N.Y.: Malamud-Rose Publishers, 1983.

Mosley, Leonard:
The Cat and the Mice. New York: Harper & Brothers Publishers, 1958.
The Druid. New York: Atheneum, 1981.

New York State Historical Association, *New York: A Guide to the Empire State.* New York: Oxford University Press, 1940.

O'Connor, Richard, *The German-Americans: An Informal History.* Boston: Little, Brown, 1968.

Paine, Lauran, *German Military Intelligence in World War II: The Abwehr.* New York: Military Heritage Press, 1984.

Peis, Günter, *The Mirror of Deception.* Transl. by William Steedman. London: Weidenfeld and Nicolson, 1977.

Perrault, Gilles, *The Red Orchestra.* Transl. by Peter Wiles and Len Ortzen.

London: Arthur Barker, 1968.

Piekalkiewicz, Janusz, *Secret Agents, Spies and Saboteurs.* Transl. by Francisca Garvie and Nadia Fowler. London: William Morrow, 1973.

Popov, Dusko, *Spy/Counterspy.* New York: Grosset & Dunlap Publishers, 1974.

Rachlis, Eugene, *They Came to Kill: The Story of Eight Nazi Saboteurs in America.* New York: Random House, 1961.

Rout, Leslie B., Jr., and John F. Bratzel, *The Shadow War: German Espionage and United States Counterespionage in Latin America during World War II.* Frederick, Md.: University Publications of America, 1986.

Schellenberg, Walter, *The Labyrinth.* Transl. by Louis Hagen. New York: Harper & Brothers Publishers, 1956.

Schulze-Holthus, Bernhard, *Daybreak in Iran: A Story of the German Intelligence Service.* Transl. by Mervyn Savill. London: Staples Press, 1954.

Skorzeny, Otto, *Skorzeny's Special Missions.* London: Robert Hale, 1957.

Stanley, Roy M., II, *World War II Photo Intelligence.* New York: Charles Scribner's Sons, 1981.

Trepper, Leopold, *The Great Game: Memoirs of the Spy Hitler Couldn't Silence.* New York: McGraw-Hill, 1988.

West, Nigel:
MI5: British Security Service Operations 1909-1945. London: The Bodley Head, 1981.
A Thread of Deceit: Espionage Myths of World War II. New York: Random House, 1985.

White, William, *Subminiature Photography.* Boston: Focal Press, 1990.

Whitehead, Don, *The FBI Story: A Report to the People.* New York: Random House, 1956.

Whiting, Charles, *Skorzeny.* New York: Ballantine Books, 1972.

Wighton, Charles, *Heydrich: Hitler's Most Evil Henchman.* Philadelphia: Chilton Company—Book Division, 1962.

Wighton, Charles, and Günter Peis, *Hitler's Spies and Saboteurs.* New York: Henry Holt, 1958.

Other Publications

U.S. Department of Justice, Criminal Division, "Outline of Evidence: German-American Bund." Washington, D.C.: U.S. Department of Justice, September 17, 1942.

Index

Prague, *160*; and Naujocks, *27*, 29; Raeder, dislike for, 19; and Salon Kitty, 29; and Schellenberg, 8, 162; Tukhachevsky affair, 25-26

Heyer, Herbert von: 76, 79

Himmler, Heinrich: and Canaris, 4, 28, 162-164, 166, 174; as chief of all German police, 22; communications intelligence, 126; Gestapo tranferred to, 14; and Heydrich, 6, 15, 19; intelligence service, overall command of, 166; and "intensified interrogation," 135; Mussolini rescue mission, 151; Operation North Pole, 121; operations in Netherlands, 110; and Red Orchestra, 137; and Schellenberg, 8, 162-165; and Skorzeny, 169

Hippel, Theodor von: 153, *154-155*

Hitler, Adolf: 75; aid to Franco's Nationalists, 30; American industrial capacity, 36, 53; Ardennes offensive, 173, 176; and Blomberg, 26-27; Blood Purge, 14-15; and Brandenburgers, 158; campaign of racial and political annihilation, 159; and Canaris, 18, 21, 38, 162, 164, 166; and counterintelligence, 112, 116, 117, 127, 136; dismantles Abwehr, 166-168; foreign expansion plans of, 15, 26, 155; and Fritsch, 28; and German-American Bund, 31; and Gibraltar, 100; and Great Britain, 67, 70, 82; ignores intelligence on Stalingrad, 87; invasion of Poland, 39; and Kaltenbrunner, 163; and Mussolini, 150-151; and Nazi bureaucracy, 125; plots against, 8, 109, 110-112, 115, 162, 174; rearmament plans of, 21; and Red Orchestra, 136; and Skorzeny, 165, 169, 170, 173; tensions with generals, 135, 174; transfers Gestapo to SS, 14; Tukhachevsky affair, 26; underestimation of Red Army, 85

Hoboken, New Jersey: 36

Hodgkins, Dana: 67

Hodgkins, Harvard: *67*

Hoettl, Wilhelm: 30, 35, 169

Hofmann, Johanna: *46, 50*

Holl, Hans: 78

Honsfeld: German troops advance at, *180*

Hoover, J. Edgar: 56, 60

Horthy, Nicholas von: 170, 171, *172*

Horthy, Niki: 170, 171, 173

Hull (England): 35

Hungary: Skorzeny's coup d'état in, 170-173

I

Interallié spy ring: 113, 115

Iran: German aerial reconnaissance in, *103*; SS operations in, 164-165

Iraq: German operatives in, 89

Ireland Aircraft Corporation: 36

Istanbul: 166

Italy: collapse of Fascist state in, 150; diplomatic codes, 125; signs armistice

with Allies, 166; support for Abwehr activities, 80

J

Jablunkov Pass: 38

Jacksonville, Florida: 53, 57

Jahnke, Felix: *50*

Jamaica, New York: 56

Japan: diplomatic codes, 125; operatives in Moscow, 87; relations with Brazil, 79

Jodl, Alfred: 70, 161

Jordan, Franz Walther: 78

K

Kaltenbrunner, Ernst: *163*, 164, 168

Kanáris, Konstantínos: 18

Kapp, Wolfgang: 16

Kappe, Walther: 53-54

Kauders, Fritz: 87

Keitel, Wilhelm: 166, 168

Kempter, Friedrich: 77, 78, 79, 80

Kent, Edward (Sukolov-Gurevich alias): 131, 132, 134, *135*, 136

Kerling, Edward: *54*

Kessler, Joe (Ludwig alias): 60

Kieffer, Josef: 118

Kiel: 35

Klausen, Olaf: 73, 74, 75, 76

Klein, Josef: *47*

Knemeyer, Siegfried: 96

Koch, Erich: 84

Koedel, Marie: 63

Koedel, Simon Emil: 63

Königsberg: Abwehr outstation in, 38

Kraemer, Karl-Heinz: 82

Kriegsmarine: 35

Krueger, Otto: 35-36

Kruger, Bernhard: 167

Kuhn, Fritz: 31, *32*

L

La Guardia Airport: 47

Lahousen, Erwin: 30-35, 38, 57

Lang, Heinz: 80-82

Lang, Hermann: 37-38, *45*, 49, 51, 62

Lauwers, Hubert: 119-120, *121*

Lawrence, T. E.: 153

League of Nations: plebiscite in Saarland, 21

Lebanon: German operatives in, 89

Leningrad: German aerial reconnaissance of, *96-97*

Lettow-Vorbeck, Paul von: 153

Lidice: Nazi reprisals in, 161

Liebknecht, Karl: 16

Linz: 163

Lisbon: 8, 46, 60, 63, 66, 67, 75

London: 35, 72, 73

Long Island: U-boats land agents on, 53-55

Long Island Railroad: 56

Lonkowski, Wilhelm: 36, 37, 42, 48

Lorient (France): U-boat base at, 54

Louisville, Kentucky: 53

Ludwig, Kurt Frederick: 58-60, *61*, 63

Luftreise (magazine): 36

Luftwaffe: aerial reconnaissance, 96, *97-107*; attempted rescue of Masri Pasha, 82; bombsight developed from Norden plans, 38, 45; ciphers of, 146; formal existence announced, 21; and Operation Sea Lion, 70; radio intelligence operations, 120, 125, 126, 127, 129; rescue of Mussolini, 149-151; Russian agents in, 134; in Spanish Civil War, 30; used to infiltrate agents, 66, *73*

Luxembourg: 176

Luxemburg, Rosa: 16

Lvov: 158

M

Madison Square Garden: German-American Bund rally at, *31-35*, 36

Madrid: 16, 18, 67

Magnitogorsk: 165

Marseilles: 115, 136

Masri Pasha: 82-83

Massena, New York: 53

Mauthausen concentration camp: 121

Max (agent): 87

Meier, Carl: 71

Meuse River: 120, 157, 158, 176-177, 180, 182

Mexico City: Abwehr networks in, 80

Mezenen, René: *47*

MI-5: 74, 75

MI-6: 35-36, 109, 119

Miami, Florida: 59, 60

Middle East: German operatives in, 21, 82-84, *89-95*

Minox: German spy camera and equipment, *22-23*

Monkaster, Peter: *90*, 91, 94, *95*

Montreal: German targets in, *58*

Moscow: 129; German aerial reconnaissance of, *102*; German operatives in, 85, 87

Mugge, Karl: 78

Müller, Hans: 83, 84

Müller, Heriberto: 77, 78

Munich: 58, 83, 110

Mussolini, Benito: 80; rescue of, 149-151

N

Nasser, Gamal Abdel: 82

Natal (Brazil): 76, 77, 78, 80

National Socialist German Workers' party: *See* Nazi party

Naujocks, Alfred: 19, 25, 39; and Heydrich, 27, 29

Navy: code-breaking activity by, 128-129; interservice rivalry in, 15; secret weaponry, *168, 169*

Navy high command: military intelligence and, *143*

Nazi party: bureaucratic rivalry in, 4, 112, 125-126, 129; growing political base of, 28

Netherlands: British operatives in, 35-36, 109-110, 112; German conquest of, 70, 112, 157; Red Orchestra in, 132

Neubauer, Hermann: *55*

Time Life Inc. offers a wide range of fine recordings, including a *Rock 'n' Roll Era* series. For subscription information, call 1-800-621-7026 or write Time-Life Music, P.O. Box C-32068, Richmond, Virginia 23261-2068.